2007

THE MARINER'S BOOK of DAYS

PETER H. SPECTRE

Sheridan House

Thanks to those who helped with the creation of this work:
Lothar Simon, Janine Simon, Kathleen Brandes, and Lindy Gifford.

Published 2006 by
Sheridan House Inc.
145 Palisade Street
Dobbs Ferry, NY 10522
www.sheridanhouse.com

Compass Rose, 4 Patten Point Road
Spruce Head, Maine 04859

Design by Sherry Streeter and Lindy Gifford

Cover art: *Working the Hudson* by Patrick O'Brien

Printed in China

ISBN 1-57409-226-X

There is no passion that man has sung
Like the love of the deep-souled Sea,
Whose tide responds to the Moon's soft light
With marvelous melody,—
For the Sea is a harp, and the winds of God
Play over his rhythmic breast,
And bear on the sweep of their mighty wings
The song of a vast unrest.

—from "A Sea Lyric," by William Hamilton Hayne

"The time has come," the Walrus said,
"To talk of many things:
Of shoes—and ships—and sealing-wax—
Of cabbages—and kings—
And why the sea is boiling hot—
And whether pigs have wings."
—Lewis Carroll

Care was lifted from our shoulders, for we were free from advice, pessimism, officialism, heat and hot air.
—K. Adlard Coles

It is remarkable how quickly a good and favorable wind can sweep away the maddening frustrations of shore living.
—Ernest K. Gann

GETTING UNDERWAY—REPORTS FROM THE FORECASTLE GANG

"Anchor's at short stay"—the vessel has been pulled up to the anchor, which still lies on the bottom.

"Anchor's up and down"—the anchor flukes have broken free, but the crown is still touching the bottom.

"Anchor's aweigh"—the anchor is no longer touching the bottom, and the vessel is underway.

WE ARE FREE

The breeze sits in the shoulder of our peak, the crisp curl of the lapping wavelet bubbles past the stem, there is an air of brisk impatience in the flapping mainsail, the taut shrouds hum with a merry air, the jib is blowing free, the warp is cast off, the rattling of the ropes and sails grows suddenly quiet, each sheet is stretched, the sails are swelling to the wind, a satisfying calm steals over our minds as the curling eddies astern tell of the gathering speed of our tidy little craft. We feel we are running out to freedom and the vague unknown. —Frank Cowper

THE NORWEGIAN STEAM SCHOONER *FRAM*, NEAR THE ANTARCTIC CIRCLE, SOUTHERN OCEAN, JANUARY 1, 1911

We said good-bye to 1910 in all friendliness over a good glass of toddy in the evening, and wished each other all possible luck in 1911. At three in the morning of New Year's Day the officer of the watch called me with news that the first iceberg was in sight. I had to go up and see it. Yes, there it lay, far to windward, shining like a castle in the rays of the morning sun. It was a big, flat-topped berg of the typical Antarctic form. It will perhaps seem paradoxical when I say that we all greeted this first sight of the ice with satisfaction and joy; an iceberg is usually the last thing to gladden sailors' hearts, but we were not looking at the risk just then. The meeting with the imposing colossus had another significance that had a stronger claim on our interest—the pack-ice could not be far off.

—Roald Amundsen

All hands unmoor! proclaims a boisterous cry.
—William Falconer

JANUARY

Monday
1
NEW YEAR'S DAY

1897—The first edition of *Jane's Fighting Ships*, a reference volume covering naval ships around the world, was published by Fred T. Jane.

Tuesday
2

1866—John MacGregor's first canoe book, *A Thousand Miles in the Rob Roy Canoe on Twenty Lakes and Rivers of Europe*, the inspiration for hundreds of voyages in double-paddle canoes, was published in England.

Wednesday ○
3

1870—Construction began on the Brooklyn Bridge over the East River, New York City.

Thursday
4

1967—Donald Malcolm Campbell achieved the highest speed on the water to date, 328 mph, on Coniston Water, Cumbria, England, in the speedboat *Bluebird K7;* seconds later, the boat disintegrated and Campbell was killed.

Friday
5

1922—Sir Ernest Shackleton, Antarctic explorer, leader of the famed *Endurance* expedition, died at Grytviken, South Georgia Island, where he is buried.

Saturday
6

1905—The first blessing of the sponge divers' fleet by the Greek Orthodox Church was held in Tarpon Springs, Florida.

Sunday
7

1807—Responding to Napoleon's announcement of a blockade of the British Isles, the Royal Navy established a blockade of continental Europe.

RED FLAGS WHEN CONSIDERING A BOAT FOR PURCHASE

Mismatched paint—could be an indication of recent damage and repair.

Musty smell—excess moisture from leaks; poor ventilation.

Scum lines higher in the bilge than expected, or on the engine block, or on bulkheads—the boat may have taken on water.

Discoloration under plumbing fixtures or pipe joints—could be a slow leak in plumbing.

Water stains around hatches, windows, and doors—seals could be bad; bedding compound might have become hard; frame could be rotten or out of alignment.

Seacocks won't open and close smoothly—they are becoming corroded.

Rusty engine—it could have been under water.

Engine oil or transmission fluid is black, or feels gritty, or has an odd smell—engine problems.

Excessive engine vibration when running—shaft could be bent or out of alignment; shaft bearings could be worn; engine bed or hold-down bolts could be loose.

Bent or dinged-up prop—may have hit an obstruction; check prop shaft for trueness; look for possible damage to the hull or keel.

Blisters on fiberglass hull—problems within the laminate.

Soft spots in deck—fiberglass: could be problems within the laminate or in the core; wood: likely to be rot.

Fin keel out of true—boat may have gone aground or fallen from slings when hauled, putting strain on keelbolts.

Hull identification number not crisp—could have been modified.

PREJUDICE IS WITH US ALWAYS, SAYS GILBERT KLINGEL

Sailboat men look down on powerboats; powerboat people view with pity the poor sailing craft becalmed or idling in a near-dead sea; the racing skipper considers the cruising yacht with disdain; the owner of a ketch wouldn't trade for a cutter twice the size; and Cleopatra's barge wouldn't interest the owner of a Chinese junk, even with the Queen of the Nile aboard. The list of preferences and prejudices is endless. It applies to rigs and rigging, to modern design versus the traditional, to every facet of boating. But most of all, strong preferences and prejudices are expressed about the materials of boat construction.

THE WHALESHIP *HENRY*, SOUTH PACIFIC OCEAN, JANUARY 8, 1822

Continues with light breeses & pleasant weather. At daylight sot the Top Gallantsails, MainSail & Flying-Jib & commenced the day with washing & scrubbing the decks. At 8 AM tacked Ship & stood to the Northward & Eastward. At 11 AM the Planter sot a signal for gamming. Took in Fore & Mizen Top Gallantsails & Flying-Jib & ran down to her, when our Captain went on board of her to spend the day & there Mate come on board of here. This day had hunt in our berths after Bed bugs & found a great many of those Birds. Ever since we came on the Coast of Peru we have been troubled with large quantities of Fleas till within a fiew weeks past thay have left us, after being relieved by severall Regimints of Bed Bugs who appear to be good Troops & lay hold of us solid.

—George Attwater

All sailors advance through the yachting scene in a fairly regular pattern—they eventually want a bigger boat.
—Carl Lane

JANUARY

Monday
8

1968—The first undersea television special produced by Jacques-Yves Cousteau, underwater documentarian and co-inventor of the Aqua-Lung, was aired.

Tuesday
9

1806—Admiral Lord Nelson's body, which had been preserved in a cask of spirits since the Battle of Trafalgar, was interred in St. Paul's Cathedral, London, England.

Wednesday
10

1791—The Portland Head Light, Portland, Maine, was illuminated for the first time.

Thursday ◑
11

1757—Alexander Hamilton, father of the U.S. Coast Guard, was born in Charles Town, the island of Nevis, West Indies.

Friday
12

1674—King Charles II of England issued a royal warrant employing the Willem Van de Veldes, the Elder and the Younger, for "taking and making Draughts of seafights."

Saturday
13

1888—The National Geographic Society was founded in Washington, DC.

Sunday
14

1969—A rocket warhead accidentally exploded aboard the aircraft carrier USS *Enterprise* in the Pacific Ocean near Hawaii; 27 lives were lost, 15 aircraft were destroyed by fire.

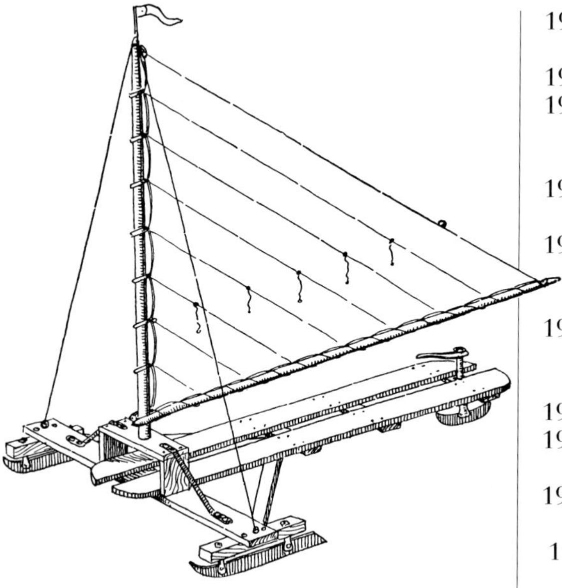

ANNALS OF ICEBOATING

Mid-17th century—iceboats first used for carrying cargo, Dutch canals
1790—first iceboat in North America, Hudson River, New York
1861—first iceboat club in North America, Poughkeepsie Ice Yacht Club, Hudson River, New York
1870—largest iceboat built: 68 feet 11 inches long, 1,070-square-foot sail area
1871—ice yacht *Icicle* beat the Chicago Express train between Poughkeepsie and Ossining, New York
1879—iceboat *Zephyr* ran the 9¾ miles from Poughkeepsie to New Hamburg on the Hudson River, New York, in seven minutes flat
1881—races for the Ice Yacht Challenge Pennant of America first held by the Orange Lake Ice Yacht Club, Hamburg, New York
1903—races begun for the Stuart Cup for iceboats with sail areas over 600 square feet
1904—Hearst Trophy, deeded by William Randolph Hearst, established for 45-foot stern-steerers
1913—*Iceboating*, edited by Herbert L. Stone, was published
1933—Walter Beauvois designed the front-steering *Beau-Skeeter*
1936—a design competition sponsored by the *Detroit News* newspaper led to the DN iceboat
1937—first DN constructed
1938—a stern-steerer on Lake Winnebago, Wisconsin, was clocked at 143 mph
1939—International Skeeter Association established
1947—Renegade Skeeter designed
1951—Eastern Ice Yachting Association took over sponsorship of the Ice Yacht Challenge Pennant of America
1953—International DN Ice Yacht Racing Association established
1954—first annual International DN Ice Yacht Racing Association regatta held, Lake St. Clair, Michigan
1960—Jane Pegel won the annual International DN Ice Yacht Racing Association regatta, the first woman to do so
1963—National Iceboat Authority established
1969—epoxy glue first used by the Gougeon brothers to build DNs
1973—first DN Gold Cup regatta, Gull Lake, Michigan
1977—Skeeter iceboat *Warrior* set a new speed record: 148 mph, on Lake Monona, Wisconsin
2003—iceboat *Das Boot* set a speed to record to date of 155.84 mph, on Lake Monona, Wisconsin

The first rule of iceboating: In the event the wind dies, never sail farther than you're willing to walk across a cold, frozen lake. —anon.

THE ISLAND OF TRISTAN DA CUNHA, SOUTH ATLANTIC OCEAN, JANUARY 1909

January 15. Soon after four this morning the settlement was awakened by terrific cries of "Sail, ho!" Some smoke was seen, and it was first thought to be that of a steamer, but there was so much it seemed to be a ship on fire. The men went off and did not get back till the evening, as they had a long distance to go. The ship was a whaler melting the blubber of a whale caught the night before. They had on deck the half of the head, inside of which men were digging with spades—which gives an idea of its size. The whale in Tristan waters is the Southern Right Whale.

January 16. A vessel emerged from the mist to-day. In a marvelously short time the men were off to her. She was a Norwegian one bound for Australia, and had made a quick run of fourteen days from Rio de Janeiro. After the men returned in the evening they had to go off again with sheep and potatoes to the whaler, which was standing out to the east.

—K. M. Barrow

The whole ocean is made up of single drops.
—Italian proverb

JANUARY

Monday
15 MARTIN LUTHER KING DAY

1947—Lieutenant James A. Cornish became the first U.S. Coast Guard helicopter pilot to fly from a ship, the USCGC *Northwind*, to the Little America base in Antarctica.

Tuesday
16

1944—Lieutenant Stewart R. Graham became the first person in a helicopter to take off from and land on a ship underway at sea, the SS *Daghestan* in the North Atlantic Ocean.

Wednesday
17

1773—The sailing ship *Resolution*, Captain James Cook, Royal Navy, became the first vessel to cross the Antarctic Circle, at 66 degrees 33 minutes S.

Thursday
18

1911—Eugene B. Ely became the first aviator to both land on and take off from a ship, the armored cruiser USS *Pennsylvania*, anchored in San Francisco Bay.

Friday ●
19

2003—The iceboat *Das Boot* set a sailing speed record on ice of 155.84 mph on Lake Monona, Wisconsin.

Saturday
20

1914—The first school for training U.S. naval aviators was established in Pensacola, Florida.

Sunday
21

1850—The passenger steamer *Arctic*, of the Collins Line, winner of the eastbound Blue Riband, was launched.

WYNKEN, BLYNKEN, AND NOD (DUTCH LULLABY)

by Eugene Field

Wynken, Blynken, and Nod one night
Sailed off in a wooden shoe—
Sailed on a river of crystal light,
Into a sea of dew.
"Where are you going, and what do you wish?"
The old moon asked the three.
"We have come to fish for the herring fish
That live in this beautiful sea;
Nets of silver and gold have we!"
Said Wynken,
Blynken,
And Nod.

The old moon laughed and sang a song,
As they rocked in the wooden shoe,
And the wind that sped them all night long
Ruffled the waves of dew.
The little stars were the herring fish
That lived in that beautiful sea—
"Now cast your nets wherever you wish—
Never afeard are we";
So cried the stars to the fishermen three:
Wynken,
Blynken,
And Nod.

All night long their nets they threw
To the stars in the twinkling foam—
Then down from the skies came the wooden shoe,
Bringing the fishermen home;
'T was all so pretty a sail it seemed
As if it could not be,
And some folks thought 't was a dream they'd dreamed
Of sailing that beautiful sea—
But I shall name you the fishermen three:
Wynken,
Blynken,
And Nod.

Wynken and Blynken are two little eyes,
And Nod is a little head,
And the wooden shoe that sailed the skies
Is a wee one's trundle-bed.
So shut your eyes while mother sings
Of wonderful sights that be,
And you shall see the beautiful things
As you rock in the misty sea,
Where the old shoe rocked the fishermen three:
Wynken,
Blynken,
And Nod.

AN EXPLANATION FOR DUTCH EXCELLENCE IN SEAMANSHIP

It is not the form or shape of our ships which makes us here in Holland excel on the water. It is our ability to sail our vessels successfully with a comparatively small crew, it is the sober way of living of these men, once on board their craft, and the innate cleanliness of our people which gives our ships a longer lease on life than those of any other nation.

THE U.S. PRIVATEER *AMERICA*, ATLANTIC OCEAN NEAR BRITISH ISLES, JANUARY 27, 1814

At 4 P. M. saw a sail on the lee bow. Made a signal for our boats and all hands to repair on board. Instantly got in the boats and made all necessary sail in chase. At 5 nearing the chase very fast. At half past 9 lighted our side lanterns and called all hands to quarters. At 10 within gunshot of him; Fired and brought him to. Got out the gig and brought the captain on board with his papers. She proved to be the British ship *Falcon*, Atkinson, master, from Liverpool via Lisbon, bound to the Canaries, with a very valuable cargo of merchandise. At 11 took on board the prisoners. Put on board Mr. Cleaves as prize master with 12 hands.

—Captain Joseph Ropes

Enough blue in the sky to make a Dutchman's breeches
And it'll be clear.
—old weather saying

JANUARY

Monday
22

1961—The Portuguese passenger liner *Santa Maria* was hijacked off Curaçao by terrorists seeking the overthrow of Portuguese dictator Antonio Salazar; the passengers were freed 11 days later in Brazil.

Tuesday
23

1960—The U.S. Navy bathyscaph *Trieste*, piloted by Jacques Piccard and Donald Walsh, reached a record depth of 35,797 feet in the Challenger Deep of the Mariana Trench southwest of Guam.

Wednesday
24

1942—The submarine S-26 sank after colliding with the submarine chaser *PC-460*, both of the U.S. Navy, in the Gulf of Panama.

Thursday ◐
25

1616—The Straits of Le Maire, between Staten Island and Tierra del Fuego near Cape Horn, were discovered by Dutch explorers Willem Cornelius Schouten and Jakob Le Maire.

Friday
26

1914—The Vanderbilt family's steam yacht *Warrior* went aground near Savanilla, Colombia. Despite dangerous sea conditions, all passengers were taken off safely.

Saturday
27

1871—The steamer *Kensington* collided with the bark *Templar* off Cape Hatteras, North Carolina; both vessels and many lives were lost.

Sunday
28

1915—The four-masted bark *William P. Frye*, the first U.S. ship to be lost in World War I, was sunk by a German cruiser in the South Atlantic off Brazil.

The Owl and the Pussy-cat went to sea
In a beautiful pea green boat,
They took some honey, and plenty of money,
Wrapped up in a five pound note.
The Owl looked up to the stars above,
And sang to a small guitar,
"O lovely Pussy! O Pussy my love,
What a beautiful Pussy you are,
You are,
You are!
What a beautiful Pussy you are!"

—Edward Lear

ANIMALS AT SEA

Bee—a piece of wood with a hole in it, fixed to the side of a spar and used as a fairlead
Blue pigeon—a hand lead used for taking soundings
Buffalo rail—a low rail at the forecastle deck
Bull's eye—a deadeye block with only one hole
Camel—a buoyant device used to lift a ship over a shallow bar
Cat—catamaran
Crab—a small capstan or winch
Crane—a hoist or derrick
Crow's nest—lookout station, usually high on the foremast
Dog—a fitting for making a door or hatch watertight
Dolphin—a piling or a cluster of piles used for mooring a vessel
Donkey engine—an auxiliary engine for powering winches and pumps
Fish—to repair a broken or split spar by lashing wooden splints alongside
Fly—the part of a flag opposite the hoist; also the word for a flag's length
Hog—keelson of a wooden boat
Horse—a metal rod on which a sail's sheet traveler rides
Mare's tails—clouds with feathery edges
Monkey—a kid or container for grog
Mule—fore-and-aft sail set on the backstay of a yawl or ketch
Otter trawl—funnel-shaped fishing net pulled by a dragger
Pelican hook—a hinged hook held shut with a link
Pig boat—submarine
Ram—a protrusion on the lower part of the stem of a naval vessel
Sheepshank—a knot used to shorten a line
Turtle deck—a deck with extreme camber or convexness
Wildcat—the barrel of a windlass

THE TEA CLIPPER *STRATHMORE*, MIN RIVER, CHINA, FEBRUARY 1857

1 Feb. Got underweigh and brought down the river, native pilot on board and 23 tow boats to assist, it being very difficult to get ships down the river Min at noon. Anchored at Quantoa in 5½ fathoms.

2 Feb. Proceeded down the river at 7 am and at noon anchored at Sharp Peak; discharged the inside pilot and tow boats. 8 set the anchor watch.

3 Feb. Daylight got underweigh; wind N by E, fine breeze. At 8 am got outside the bar. Outside pilot left. Made sail. Strong breeze.

—Captain John Mann

The Sea yeelds Action to the bodie, Meditation to the Minde.
—Samuel Purchas

JAN/FEB

Monday
29

1888—English poet Edward Lear, best known for "The Owl and the Pussy-cat," died in San Remo, Italy.

Tuesday
30

1997—The largest ship propeller to date—six blades, 25.5 feet in diameter—was cast by Stone Manganese Marine Ltd. of the United Kingdom

Wednesday
31

1952—The movie *Sailor Beware*, a comedy starring Dean Martin and Jerry Lewis, opened in theaters across America.

Thursday
1

1788—The first United States patent for a steamboat was issued by the state of Georgia to Isaac Briggs and William Longstreet.

Friday ○
2
GROUNDHOG DAY

1914—Establishment of the United States Power Squadrons occurred during a conference at the New York Yacht Club, New York City.

Saturday
3

1966—The United States launched the first weather satellite, ESSA-1, into earth orbit.

Sunday
4

1937—A crippling longshoremen's strike ended in San Francisco.

A shipmaster might sail for a lifetime without once meeting the ideal combination of conditions for attaining the full potential speed of his ship.

—Carl Cutler

VENDEE GLOBE CHALLENGE, NONSTOP SINGLEHANDED AROUND THE WORLD, WESTWARD, BEGINNING AND ENDING AT LES SABLES D'OLONNE, FRANCE

1990—*Ecureuil D'Aquitaine II:* Titouan Lamazou, France; 109 days, 8 hours, 48 minutes
1993—*Bagages Superior;* Alain Gautier, France; 110 days, 2 hours, 22 minutes
1997—*Geodis;* Christophe Auguin, France; 105 days, 20 hours, 31 minutes
2001—*PRB;* Michel Desjoyeaux, France; 93 days
2003—*IDEC*; Francis Joyon, France; 72 days, 22 hours, 54 minutes
2005—B&*Q;* Ellen MacArthur, Britain; 71 days, 14 hours, 18 minutes

THE RACING RULES, ACCORDING TO ALBERT STRANGE

Some rules are so bad initially that they soon bring about their own downfall, and any rule, however good it may seem at birth, will be certain to be so manipulated by clever designers that speed will be obtained at the expense of all other qualities. Nearly all rules begin by producing desirable boats (a cheering assurance of the continuing sanity of the human mind), but all end by so modifying the desirable boat that she becomes undesirable as a cruiser.

I'm not particularly interested in racing or record passages. After all, I go to sea to get away from the competitive rat-race, not to join it.

—James Wharram

THE CLIPPER SHIP *SEA SERPENT*, ATLANTIC OCEAN EAST OF NEW JERSEY, FEBRUARY 10, 1855

O misery! last night was awful, so cold I thought I should freeze; and sleeting; every rope like a bar of iron. Toward daylight made a sail, set close-reefed fore- and mizzen topsails and close-reefed spanker. At 8 A.M. set reefed mainsail. At 8:30 passed two sail, a bark under close-reefed topsails and a brigantine hove to under main staysail. Snow fell several times during the morning, but luckily not in any quantity. During the morning shook reef out of foresail and fore- and main topsails and set jib. At 3 P.M. shook a reef out of mizzen topsail and spanker. Towards night the wind began to die away. At 8 P.M. reefed foresail, furled spanker and jib. Wind light, at 11 P.M. set spanker and jib. Heading all night W, W ½ N.

—Hugh McCulloch Gregory

Many a race has been won by knowing the currents and tides and taking advantage of them.
—A. Hyatt Verrill

FEBRUARY

Monday
5

1941—The cargo ship *Politician*, with 22,000 cases of whiskey, ran aground on Eriskay Island, Outer Hebrides, an event that became the basis of the comic novel *Whisky Galore*, by Compton Mackenzie.

Tuesday
6

1922—The Washington Naval Treaty, which placed limitations on the navies of the United States, Britain, Japan, France, and Italy, was signed in Washington, DC.

Wednesday
7

2005—Ellen MacArthur, in the trimaran *B&Q*, set a record to date for the fastest singlehanded nonstop circumnavigation of the globe—71 days, 14 hours, 18 minutes, 33 seconds—beating the old record by more than a day.

Thursday
8

1921—Colin Archer, designer of the Norwegian *redningsskoites* (rescue boats), on which so many cruising boats have been based, died in Larvik, Norway.

Friday
9

1759—The first commercial wharf was built in Savannah, Georgia.

Saturday ◐
10

1807—The Coast Survey, charged with charting the coastline of the United States, was established by an Act of Congress.

Sunday
11

1688—Edward Lloyd's Coffee House, which would eventually become Lloyd's of London, the world center of maritime insurance, opened.

Under the shadow of the berg.

THE TERMINOLOGY OF SEA ICE

Ice rind—thin ice close inshore where freshwater overrides saltwater
Sheet ice—smooth, level, new ice
Pan ice—small sheet
Pancake ice—a small sheet whose edges have become built up higher than the center
Rafted ice—cakes of ice have ridden up on each other
Field ice—ice that has broken away from bays and rivers and is adrift at sea
Floe—a small field
Hummock ice—chunks that have been thrown up in piles from the impact of two fields coming together
Anchor ice—ice that extends all the way to the sea bottom
Drift ice—discrete pieces that have broken from a field
Floe ice—drift ice that has come together and frozen into a small field
Pack ice—a mass of broken floes that have become frozen together
Land ice—floating ice attached to the shore
Sludge (aka brash)—field or drift ice that has become broken up and slushy
Lolly—small pieces of broken ice with slush between
Slob ice—slushy ice created by newly fallen snow
Calving—the process by which icebergs are made, by breaking off from glaciers
Blink—a glow on the horizon caused by light reflected from ice fields over the horizon

THE RESEARCH BARK *SCOTIA*, NEARING WEDDELL SEA, ANTARCTICA, FEBRUARY 18, 1903

To-day we crossed the Antarctic Circle in an open sea with only three small weathered icebergs in sight. The wind was fresh all day, and a goodly sea running, truly oceanic in character. For several hours at a time, during the last three days, we have sailed through water entirely free from ice of any description; and during other times have passed only stray bergs, mostly very weathered specimens and small in size, hardly any of them being of the real flat-topped type. What a change from our struggles further west and north, ten days or a week ago, when encountering heavy pack-ice and hammering back again northward to get rid of it, and how glad we are now that we saved our coal and our time! Men inexperienced in ice might be hammering away still. We resolved, however, not to tackle it, but to get out of it and try further east. Success thus crowned our efforts, despite our dread of possibly not getting well south.

—William Speirs Bruce

The captain had been telling how, in one of his Arctic voyages, it was so cold that the mate's shadow froze fast to the deck and had to be ripped loose by main strength. And even then he got only about two-thirds of it back.

—Mark Twain

The polar bear will make a rug
Almost as white as snow;
But if he gets you in his hug,
He rarely lets you go.

—A. T. Quiller-Couch

They say "Once bitten, twice shy" but that does not apply to Sea Fever.
—A. H. Rasmussen

FEBRUARY

Monday
12 LINCOLN'S BIRTHDAY

1935—The *Macon*, the last dirigible in the United States Navy, crashed during a storm off the coast of California; two lives were lost.

Tuesday
13

1899—The White Star liner *Germanic*, while taking on coal at New York during a blizzard, heeled over at her pier, filled with water, and sank.

Wednesday
14 VALENTINE'S DAY

1900—The U.S. Congress authorized the restoration of USS *Constitution's* hull and rigging to the condition in which it had been when she was on active duty.

Thursday
15

1946—The Inland Waterways Association, devoted to the preservation of canals for commercial and pleasure use, was established in Bloomsbury, London, England.

Friday
16

1804—The U.S. frigate *Philadelphia*, previously captured by Tripoli in the U.S. war with the Barbary pirates, was destroyed by a naval party led by Lieutenant Stephen Decatur.

Saturday ●
17

1993—Kenichi Horie arrived in Okinawa, Japan, setting a distance record to date in a pedal boat, 4,660 miles from Hawaii.

Sunday
18 CHINESE NEW YEAR (YEAR OF THE BOAR)

1942—Two U.S. Navy destroyers—USS *Truxtun* and USS *Pollux*—ran aground during a storm in Placentia Bay, Newfoundland, and were wrecked; 204 lives were lost.

Two ships may be built to exactly the same design, but the one will behave like a pig at sea all her days, while the other never gives the slightest trouble to her crew.

—T. C. Lethbridge

THE SHAPE OF THE BOW, ACCORDING TO SIR HENRY MAINWARING (1644)

If the bow be too broad the ship will not pass easily through the sea, but carry a great deal of dead water before her; if it be too lean or thin, she will beat or pitch mightily into a hollow sea for want of breadth to bear her up, so that there must be a discreet mean betwixt both these.

THE BRIG *RISING STATES*, NEAR NANTUCKET ISLAND, MASSACHUSETTS, FEBRUARY 20, 1777

At 7 AM, Saw Cape Cod from our topmast head Bearing NW Dist 7 Leags. At 11 AM, Saw the Island of Nantucket Bearg WSW. 7 Legs Dist. Struck into the SE, side of the Island for to beat to the harbour. At 1 PM, Struck on a Shoal & by the Violence of the wheather was Obligd to bare Away. Our men Was Greatly Fearg & Frost bitten. First part of these 24 hours fresh gale and a large Sea. At 3 PM The Island of Nantucket bore WNW Dist 7 Legs The South Shoal of Nantucket bore SSW. Dist 3 Legs. A fresh gail our men being Almost beat out. At 5 the gail Still Increasing tis thought by all the Officers on board, that it was Impossible to Stand the Course being So lumberd With Ice & the most of our people badly Froze twas thought proper by the Officers to bare away for Virginia.

—Captain James Thompson

HULL STRAINS

Hog—longitudinal; the ends droop
Sag—longitudinal; the midsection droops
Transverse—side-to-side; the sides are pushed in
Local—a load is unusually concentrated (i.e., from the thrust of the mast)

THE ADVANTAGES OF TUMBLEHOME (INWARD SLOPE OF THE TOPSIDES)

It reduces the area, and therefore the weight, of the deck.
A greater angle of heel is required to immerse the rail.
The mainsheet is less likely to be hung up on a sharp transom corner.

THE DISADVANTAGES OF TUMBLEHOME

Tracks and fairleads for the headsails must be located farther inboard or carried on extensions beyond the deck edge.
Unless artistically designed, it can create an ugly hull.

THE THREE TYPES OF RESISTANCE TO A YACHT'S FORWARD MOTION

Form, or wave-making resistance—caused by the shape of the hull
Surface friction—caused by the skin of the hull
Windage, or wind resistance—caused by the surface area of the topsides and rig

THE EIGHT PRINCIPAL MOTIONS OF A VESSEL AT SEA, ACCORDING TO FRANCIS S. KINNEY

Roll—tilt rhythmically from side to side
Pitch—plunge, or hobbyhorse
Heave—rise and fall
Yaw—lurch from one side of the course to the other
Surge—accelerate and decelerate with the sea swell
Sway—move from side to side
Broach—swing around when running free
Pitchpole—make a forward half-somersault

A boat is not doing her best unless there is perfect harmony between the forces acting against the hull and against the sails.
—Charles G. Davis

FEBRUARY

Monday
19 PRESIDENTS' DAY

1941—The Coast Guard Reserve was reestablished as a military arm of the U.S. Coast Guard; the old nonmilitary reservists were transferred to the new Coast Guard Auxiliary.

Tuesday
20

1966—Carl C. Cutler, maritime historian, author of *Greyhounds of the Sea* and *Queens of the Western Ocean* and a founder of Mystic Seaport Museum, died in Connecticut.

Wednesday
21 ASH WEDNESDAY

1838—Alexis-Marie Rochon, who made great improvements in the mariner's spyglass, or telescope, was born.

Thursday
22 WASHINGTON'S BIRTHDAY

1784—The *Empress of China* departed New York on the first American commercial voyage to China.

Friday
23

1879—A gale struck the coasts of New England and the maritime provinces of Canada, causing great destruction. The fishing fleet of Gloucester, Massachusetts, alone lost 17 vessels and 143 men.

Saturday ◐
24

1836—Winslow Homer, painter of hundreds of works with a marine theme, was born in Boston, Massachusetts.

Sunday
25

1862—The iron warship USS *Monitor* was commissioned at the Brooklyn Navy Yard, New York.

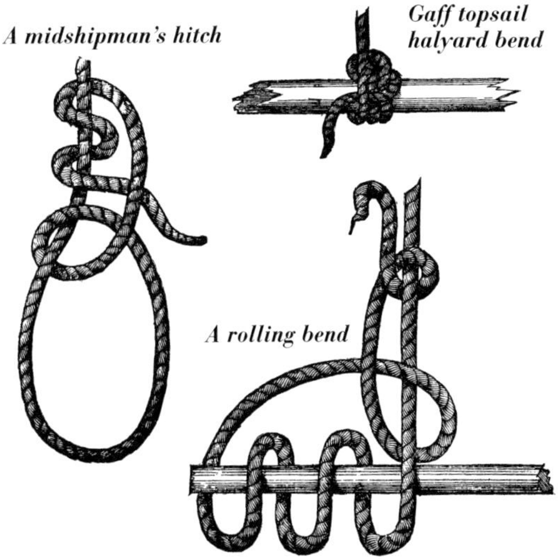

ROPEWORK MAKES THE SAILOR, SAYS RICHARD HENRY DANA, JR.

The common saying that to hand, reef and steer makes a sailor, is a mistake. It is true that no man is a sailor until he can do these things; yet to ship for an able seaman he must, in addition to these, be a good workman upon rigging .... No man will pass for an able seaman in a square-rigged vessel, who cannot make a long and short splice in a large rope, fit a block-strap, pass seizings to lower rigging, and make the ordinary knots, in a fair, workmanlike manner.

THE BRIG HMS *BEAGLE*, SOUTHWEST COAST OF CHILE, MARCH 4, 1835

We entered the harbour of Concepcion. While the ship was beating up to the anchorage, I landed on the island of Quiriquina. The mayor-domo of the estate quickly rode down to tell me the terrible news of the great earthquake of the 20th:—"That not a house in Concepcion or Talcahuano (the port) was standing; that seventy villages were destroyed; and that a great wave had almost washed away the ruins of Talcahuano." Of this latter statement I soon saw abundant proofs—the whole coast being strewed over with timber and furniture as if a thousand ships had been wrecked. Besides chairs, tables, book-shelves, etc., in great numbers, there were several roofs of cottages, which had been transported almost whole. The storehouses at Talcahuano had been burst open, and great bags of cotton, yerba, and other valuable merchandise were scattered on the shore.

—Charles Darwin

THE IDEAL KNOT

Holds fast in all conditions for the intended purpose.

Can be taken apart easily when necessary.

A knot is never "nearly right"; it is either exactly right or it is hopelessly wrong.

—Clifford Ashley

A BIBLIOGRAPHY OF KNOTS, RIGGING, AND CANVAS

The Ashley Book of Knots, by Clifford W. Ashley, 1944

Splicing Wire and Fiber Rope, by Raoul Graumont and John Hensel, 1945

The Marlinspike Sailor, by Hervey Garrett Smith, 1960

Working in Canvas, by P. W. Blandford, 1965

The Essential Knot Book, by Colin Jarman, 1984

The Rigger's Apprentice, by Brion Toss, 1985

The Splicing Handbook, by Barbara Merry, 1987

The Big Book of Boat Canvas, by Karen Lipe, 1988

The Complete Canvasworker's Guide, by Jim Grant, 1992

The Rigger's Locker, by Brion Toss, 1992

HOW TO MAKE SPUN YARN FOR WORMING, SERVING, SEIZING, ETC.

A Piece of Junk or old Cable is untwisted, the Yarns drawn out, knotted together, and rolled up in Balls round the hand. Three or four Balls are laid upon Deck, and an End out of each being taken, they are coiled in Fakes upon a Grating, or other thing (to keep the Tar from the Deck), and upon every three or four Fakes Tar is rubbed by a Brush. These are fastened by their Ends to a kind of Reel called a Spun-yarn Winch, and a half-hitch is taken over one of the Spokes. The Man who spins the Yarn, retires to a convenient distance, and then, with a brisk motion (holding the Yarns in his hands) he whirls the Winch around against the Sun [counterclockwise]. When it is spun sufficiently, he rubs it backwards and forwards, with a piece of old Canvas, which he keeps in his hand, reels it on the Winch, takes another half-hitch round the Spoke and proceeds as before. When the Reel is full, it is taken off and balled.

—*The Young Sea Officer's Sheet Anchor*, by Darcy Lever Esq., 1819

The best way to master a knot is to use it.
—Brion Toss

FEB/MARCH

Monday
26

1811—The U.S. Congress passed an act to establish naval hospitals.

Tuesday
27

1876—The New York pilot schooner *Caprice* was run down and sunk by the steamer *New Orleans* in The Narrows, New York Harbor; she was later refloated and returned to service.

Wednesday
28

1942—The Bureau of Navigation and Steamboat Inspection was transferred to the administrative control of the U.S. Coast Guard.

Thursday
1

1938—The steel sail-training bark *Admiral Karpfanger* (ex–*L'Avenir*) went missing near Cape Horn en route from Australia to Europe.

Friday
2

1770—A riot broke out at Gray's Ropewalk, which manufactured cordage for the New England shipbuilding industry, between British soldiers and citizens of Boston, Massachusetts.

Saturday ○
3

2001—The catamaran *Club Med* won an around-the-world race—aka "The Race"—in celebration of the Millennium, setting a record to date of 62 days for the distance.

Sunday
4

1394—Infante Dom Henrique, Duke of Viseu, aka Prince Henry the Navigator, was born in Portugal.

U.S. NAVY BEAN SOUP, ENOUGH FOR THE ENTIRE CREW

Beans, white, dry, 3½ quarts
Ham stock, 7 gallons
Ham bones, 8
Carrots, shredded, 2¾ cups
Onions, finely chopped
Pepper, 2 teaspoons
Flour, hard wheat, sifted, 2 cups
Water, cold, ¾ quart

Pick over and wash beans. If beans are old, soak 3 to 4 hours prior to cooking. Add ham stock and ham bones. Heat to boiling point; cover and simmer 2 to 3 hours or until beans are tender. If necessary, add hot water. Remove ham bones. Add carrots, onions, and pepper (for Old Fashioned Navy Bean Soup, add one no. 10 can of tomatoes). Simmer for 30 minutes. Blend flour and water to a smooth paste. Stir into soup, add salt and additional pepper if desired, cook 10 minutes longer.

Yield: 6¼ gallons, or 100 portions of 1 cup each

PLANKED HADDOCK, AN OLD NOVA SCOTIA RECIPE

Heat the plank (which should be of oak or maple, one and a half inches thick) very hot, then rub it over with a piece of butter or salt pork. Then spread the fish on it skin side down and brush it over well with melted butter or olive oil. Sprinkle it with salt and pepper and place in the hot oven for 20 minutes. Then arrange thin strips of bacon across the fish and return it to the oven until the bacon is crisp. Make a border of potato balls made of mashed potatoes beaten until creamy and mixed with an egg yolk all about the fish; brush these with beaten egg and milk and return to the oven to brown.

—Miss Nora E. Smith,
Halifax, Nova Scotia, 1923

COOKING LOBSTERS, ACCORDING TO JESS'S MARKET, ROCKLAND, MAINE

Put about one inch of water and a handful of salt in a pot. Bring to a rapid boil. Put in lobsters and cover. When steam comes out around edges of cover, start timing.

Hard shells

1¼ lb. size—cook 20 minutes
1½ lb. size—cook 25 to 30 minutes
3 to 4 lb. size—cook 40 to 45 minutes

Soft shells

1¼ lb. size—cook 15 minutes
1½ lb. size—cook 20 minutes

Lobsters may be reheated in microwave or by steaming again for a short time.

THE CLIPPER SHIP *DREADNOUGHT*, EASTWARD PASSAGE, NORTH ATLANTIC OCEAN, MARCH 1859

March 5.—Heavy gales and snow squalls, North to N.N.E. Distance 218 miles.

March 6.—Winds N.E. to South, light. Distance 133 miles.

March 7.—Winds S.S.E., brisk breeze and clear. Distance 282 miles.

March 8.—S.S.W. to South, fresh breeze and clear. Distance 313 miles.

March 9.—Brisk gales, South to S.E. Distance 268 miles.

March 10.—Wind S.E. to S.W., brisk breeze and squally. Distance 205 miles.

March 11.—Wind South to S.W., strong breeze and squally. Distance 308 miles.

—Captain Samuel Samuels

Note: This passage, New York to Liverpool, *Dreadnought*'s best across the Atlantic, took 13 days, 9 hours.

The best antidote to fear is food.
—Captain Edwin Campion Vaughan

MARCH

Monday
5

1883—The iron clipper ship *Cassiope* arrived in Victoria, Australia, from Calcutta, with a cargo of animals, including the first elephant imported to Australia.

Tuesday
6

1922—Cooks on the Banks fishing schooners out of Lunenburg, Nova Scotia, went on strike for more pay, paralyzing the fleet.

Wednesday
7

1867—The U.S. Congress voted a gold medal to Cyrus W. Field for his triumph in laying the first transatlantic submarine telegraphic cable.

Thursday
8

1862—The ironclad CSS *Virginia*, rebuilt from the captured wooden squarerigger USS *Merrimac*, sank the USS *Congress* and USS *Cumberland*.

Friday
9

1774—A violent wind blew down the Brant Point light tower, Nantucket Island, Massachusetts.

Saturday
10

1854—Cyrus Field's New York, Newfoundland, and London Telegraph Company, with a goal to lay the first transatlantic cable, was established.

Sunday
11

1902—Two large wooden vessels were launched on the same tide, the same day, in the little town of Essex, Massachusetts—the knockabout schooner *Helen B. Thomas*, the first of her type, and the steam fisherman *Alice M. Jacobs*.

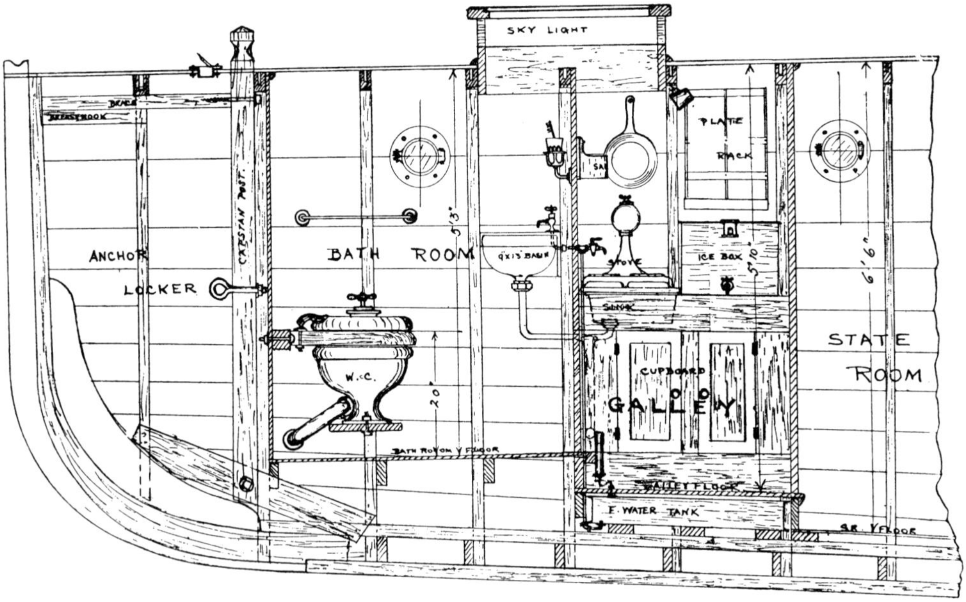

Nearly all beginners plan far too much accommodation for the dimensions of the boat they have in mind.

—Maurice Griffiths

Keep it simple and have more fun.

—Joel White

THE MOST IMPORTANT ACCOMMODATIONS UNIT OF MEASUREMENT, ACCORDING TO C. P. KUNHARDT

It is a difficult problem in all yachts how to arrange the available space to the best advantage, and the difficulty increases rapidly as the size of the yacht decreases. In comparing the relative accommodations of yachts, it is often forgotten that there is a unit of measurement for all, large or small, by which they must be gauged; and this unit is the height of a man, or say 6 ft., as the least head room in which the average man can move in comfort.

BEWARE OF GADGETS, SAYS HOWARD CHAPELLE

It is well to proceed with caution in the development of folding, sliding, and disappearing "gadgets." Many of these are very taking on paper, or in the boat while she is new, but a year or two of hard service often shows up weaknesses that lead to the discarding of these ideas. The effect of shrinking and swelling or corrosion of materials exposed to dampness is the prime cause of the downfall of many a handsome gadget.

THE CAPE COD CATBOAT MASCOT, EAST COAST OF FLORIDA, MARCH 13, 1913

Turned out at daylight again. No use for the bunk these hot, lifeless mornings. Got provisions, ice, etc., and up anchor by 10:30. "She's the Liverpool packet, My Boys, let her go." North from Palm Beach the sail along the shore is most beautiful. More flowers are in bloom than when we came down and I guess it was a "riot of color" this morning. I am mighty glad to have seen it, but am not sorry to be leaving it. When I asked a storekeeper why everybody didn't leave it, he answered, "By God they just can't. In three Years they lose all their money farming and then they 'gotter' stay." Some of these farming propositions look short of criminal. A sample of Everglades soil sent to Washington for analysis was returned to Miami with report that there was no value to it for any crop except slight trace of moisture. The old trade wind blew heavily from south, but for comfort's sake we kept awning up and let her jog along with motor. It is no joke to pile up under sail in heavy breeze and have to push, pull and kedge in blazing sun. Down past Jupiter Inlet with rushing fair tide and on into Hobe Sound.

—Henry M. Plummer

I want a boat that drinks six, eats four, and sleeps two.
—Ernest K. Gann

MARCH

Monday 12

1887—The yachts *Dauntless* and *Coronet* got underway on a great ocean race across the Atlantic Ocean from New York to Queenstown, Ireland.

Tuesday 13

2004—The unlimited hydroplane *Miss Budweiser*, driven by Dave Villwock, set a speed record to date for a propeller-driven boat of 220.493 mph at Thermalito Afterbay, Oroville, California.

Wednesday 14

1825—Samuel Samuels, one of the most famous transatlantic sailing-packet captains, for many years commander of the fast packet *Dreadnought*, skipper of the racing yacht *Henrietta*, was born in Philadelphia, Pennsylvania.

Thursday 15

1946—U.S. Coast Guard aircraft were used for the first time on the International Ice Patrol in the North Atlantic.

Friday 16

1915—W. J. Johnston, Jr., was awarded a patent on a pull-up propeller device for inboard-engine boats that came to be central to the Disappearing Propeller Motorboat (aka the Dispro).

Saturday 17 ST. PATRICK'S DAY

1848—The clipper ship *Rainbow*, one of the earliest of the type, sailed from New York for Valparaiso (Chile) and China; she was never heard from again.

Sunday 18

1848—Nathanael Greene Herreshoff, naval architect and marine engineer, was born in Bristol, Rhode Island.

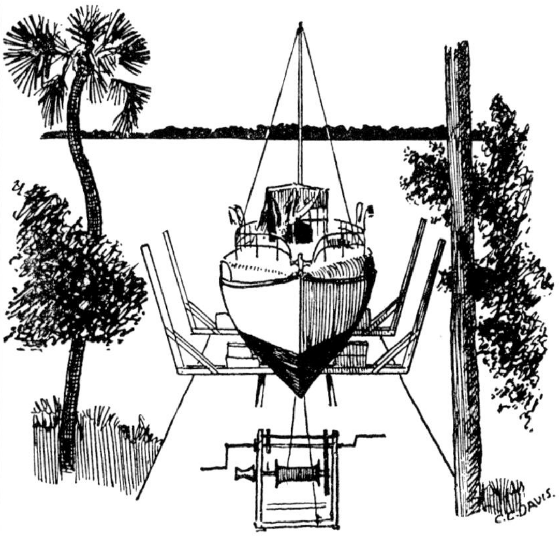

With rushing winds and gloomy skies
The dark and stubborn winter dies;
Far-off, unseen, Spring finally cries,
Bidding her earliest child arise;
March!

—Bayard Taylor

Every spring the bug hits the yachtsman, be he rich or poor, and he migrates to the water in search of those hours of labor on the boat which, to his mind, are hours of pleasant relaxation.

—Winthrop P. Moore

ADVERTISEMENT, *NORWICH MERCURY*, NORWICH, ENGLAND, MARCH 22, 1851

Fras. Clowes is favoured with Instructions from the Proprietor, to sell by auction at Rudrum's Wharf, King Street, Norwich, on Friday next, the 28th day of March, 1851, at 11 o'clock precisely, in separate lots, those two fast and favourite wherries, the *Snipe*, 28 tons burden, and the *Lapwing*, 34 tons burden, with all their masts, sails, patent winches, tarpawlings, anchors, quants, chain-hooks, purchase-gears, chain runners, and other necessary stores. The former of these Wherries was thoroughly repaired last October, and on the latter a large sum of money was expended in rebuilding her a few years since, and as the proprietor wholly declines the water carrying business, his instructions are to sell without reserve. Also a very excellent Wherry's Sail. For further particulars apply to the Auctioneer, St. Andrews Hall Plain, Norwich.

FITTING-OUT IN THE SPRING

When planning a fit-out, arrange two separate schedules: one for inside work and one for outside. Then follow one schedule or another as the weather permits. In good weather, follow the outside schedule; in foul, follow the inside.

Overlap jobs as required. While waiting for the first coat of varnish in the cabin below to dry so you can lay on the second, wash the outside deckhouse paint or polish the brass.

Before scraping and sanding any surface that has been touched by oil, grease, or wax, wash it with soogee (a cup of non-ammonia detergent and a cup of bleach in a pail of fresh, hot water) and rinse with fresh water.

Do not scrape, sand, or sweep when paint or varnish is drying nearby.

Avoid having someone scraping and sanding aloft while another is painting or varnishing on deck.

Generally speaking, scrape, sand, paint, and varnish from the top down. If the spars are stepped, begin literally at the masthead.

Below decks, generally speaking, work from the most inaccessible spaces toward the most accessible. In most boats, this will be from the forepeak aft.

If in a hurry to get her in the water, concentrate on outside, below-the-waterline work first, and anything that requires ladders, boatyard power, and a rock-steady platform. The remaining work can be done after she is launched.

I find it easier as I grow older to tell people how to do things than to go about the task myself.

—William Atkin

A sloppy, ill-kept ship is ever the mark of a poor sailor and an indication of indifference or ignorance or both.
—Hervey Garrett Smith

MARCH

Monday ●
19

1918—Daylight saving time was authorized by an Act of Congress.

Tuesday
20

1931—Gar Wood, driving his supercharged unlimited hydroplane *Miss America IX* at 102.256 mph over a one-mile course at Indian River, Florida, became the first person to break 100 mph on the water.

Wednesday
21
VERNAL EQUINOX

2003—The Cunard Line's *Queen Mary 2*, the largest passenger liner in the world to date, was launched in Saint-Nazaire, France.

Thursday
22

1933—President Franklin Delano Roosevelt signed into a law an act of the U.S. Congress legalizing the sale of beer and wine, thus sealing the fate of bootlegging at sea.

Friday
23

1776—The Continental Congress authorized privateering against British commerce.

Saturday
24

1882—Henry Wadsworth Longfellow, author of "The Building of the Ship" and other poems with a seagoing theme, died in Cambridge, Massachusetts.

Sunday ◐
25

1915—The U.S. submarine *F4* sank off Honolulu, Hawaii, after a battery exploded; 21 lives were lost.

OCCUPATIONS OF A FEW EARLY MARINE ARTISTS BEFORE THEY BECAME KNOWN FOR THEIR ART

Antonio Jacobsen—safe painter
Robert Salmon—commercial artist
Martin Johnson Heade—carriage painter
Francis Silva—sign painter
Winslow Homer—engraver
FitzHugh Lane—lithographer
John Frederick Kensett—banknote engraver
W. T. Richards—light-fixture designer
James Hamilton—book illustrator
Frederick S. Cozzens—newspaper and book illustrator
Archibald Cary Smith—yacht designer
Worthington Wittredge—house and sign painter

Never put more than two waves in a picture; it's fussy.

—Winslow Homer

THE WONDER AND POWER OF ART, ACCORDING TO GEORGE BELLOWS

When I paint the beginning of a ship…, I feel the reverence the ship builder has for his handiwork. He is creating something splendid, to master wind and wave, something as fine and powerful as Nature's own forces…. When I paint the colossal frame of the skeleton of this ship I want to put his wonder and his power into my canvas.

THE KEY TO BELIEVABLE MARINE ART, ACCORDING TO JOHN CARTER, MARITIME MUSEUM DIRECTOR

Experience is a keyword in this work, and it can be argued that the majority of our greatest marine artists, past and present, were intimately familiar with the subjects they chose to paint. It is this familiarity with the ways of a ship that breathes life into the painted surface—familiarity with the routine of shipboard life, the caress of the wind in the sails, or the throb and heat of an engineroom.

All that I desire to point out is the general principle that Life imitates Art far more than Art imitates Life.

—Oscar Wilde

THE FOUR-MASTED BARK *EDWARD SEWALL*, FIGHTING TO ROUND CAPE HORN, EAST TO WEST, 1914

March 26. More moderate but terrible heavy cross sea. Ship under water all the time.

March 27. Wind W.S.W., strong gale.

March 28. Calm to heavy N.N.W. gale.

March 29. Terrible heavy N.W. gale. Lost mizzen upper topsail and main lower topgallant sail. Got 2 men hurt. All hands on deck all night.

March 30. 6 A.M. Quick shift from N.W. to S.W. with hurricane force, with terrible heavy cross sea. Ship under 2 lower topsails and under water. Lost outer jib, washed off the boom.

March 31. Wind W.S.W. Very heavy gale.

April 1. Terrible heavy W.N.W. gale, ship under 2 lower topsails and drifting to the Eastward, and my heart is broken with those heavy gales all the time.

—Captain Richard Quick

A sailor is an artist whose medium is the wind.
—Webb Chiles

MAR/APRIL

Monday
26

2003—The U.S. Navy began using dolphins to help locate mines laid by Iraqi forces off the coast and in the waterways of Iraq.

Tuesday
27

1811—Edward William Cooke, marine artist, best known for his series of engravings published in the book *Shipping and Craft*, was born in London, England.

Wednesday
28

1793—Henry Rowe Schoolcraft, discoverer of the source of the Mississippi River, was born in Albany County, New York.

Thursday
29

1949—A British Order-in-Council abolished flogging as a form of punishment in the Royal Navy.

Friday
30

1867—A two-day storm destroyed the light tower and keeper's house at the entrance to Timbalier Bay, Louisiana.

Saturday
31

1995—The U.S. Coast Guard sent its last official radio message by Morse code.

Sunday
1

DAYLIGHT SAVING BEGINS
APRIL FOOLS' DAY / PALM SUNDAY

1778—The *Virginia*, of the fledgling Continental Navy, was captured by a British squadron.

CHOOSING A YACHT ENSIGN, RECOMMENDED SIZES

Length of Boat	Size of Yacht Ensign
Under 20 feet	12″ x 18″
20–30 feet	16″ x 24″
30–40 feet	24″ x 36″
40–70 feet	30″ x 48″
70–90 feet	36″ x 60″
90–100+ feet	48″ x 72″

THE U.S. SLOOP-OF-WAR *JAMESTOWN*, NORTH ATLANTIC OCEAN, APRIL 5, 1847

Fresh gale at south, ship going 11 to 12 knots. At 2 p.m. furled topgallant sails and single-reefed the topsails and spanker. In the evening the wind canted S.S.W. Uncle Sam's hide ropes do not stand like chains. At 10 p.m. weather threatening; called all hands and got snug by 1 a.m.; reefed down to three-reefed fore and main topsails, whole foresail, spencer and reefed spanker; split the fore topmast staysail and saved the jib with difficulty. After keeping about S.E. to get the canvas snug, we bore away to E.N.E., a large sea running and the tops occasionally coming over forward of the main rigging: the ship steers beautifully, and could not be easier in her motion. In the early morning the wind moderated; were obliged to haul up to keep her steady, and swiftered in the lower rigging until it could be set up carefully. Made 195 miles.

—Commander R. B. Forbes

DRESSING SHIP

When dressing ship—that is, flying signal flags from stem to stern during holidays and for special events, such as races and regattas—the proper sequence is more or less standard: A B 2 U J 1 K E 3 G H 6 I V 5 F L 4 D M 7 P O 3rd substitute R N 1st substitute S T 0 [zero] C X 9 W Q 8 Z Y 2nd substitute

Using all the flags and pennants is known as rainbow dressing.

SPECIAL SIGNAL FLAGS

Solid blue, starboard main spreader—owner absent

Solid blue, white diagonal stripe, starboard main spreader—owner absent, guest aboard

Solid white, starboard main spreader—owner at meal

Red pennant, port fore spreader—crew at meal (aka chow rag)

Blue pennant, main truck—night pennant

Commission pennant—signal indicating a naval or coast guard vessel is officially in commission

House flag—distinguishing flag of the company that owns a merchant or passenger vessel

GAG SIGNAL FLAGS—FLY AT YOUR PERIL

Coffeepot—open for coffee
Foaming stein—open for beer
Martini glass—open for cocktails
Bunny rabbits—crew asleep, do not disturb
Ball and chain—wife aboard
Witch riding a broomstick—wife ashore
Battle-ax—mother-in-law aboard

A thoughtful mind when it sees a nation's flag, sees not the flag only, but the nation itself.
—Henry Ward Beecher

APRIL

Monday ◯
2

1863—The U.S. Navy's first experimental submarine, under tow by USS *Sumpter* from Washington, DC, to Charleston, South Carolina, sank during a storm off Cape Hatteras, North Carolina.

Tuesday
3 PASSOVER

1783—Washington Irving, author of *The Life and Voyages of Christopher Columbus* and *The Voyages and Discoveries of the Companions of Columbus*, was born in New York City.

Wednesday
4

1818—An Act of Congress ordered that the U.S. flag have thirteen stripes and twenty stars, and that "on the admission of every new state into the Union one star be added to the union of the flag."

Thursday
5

1621—The pilgrim ship *Mayflower* sailed from Plymouth, Massachusetts, on her return trip across the Atlantic to England.

Friday
6 GOOD FRIDAY

1917—The U.S. Coast Guard, which at the time had a force of 200 officers, 5,000 enlisted personnel, and 15 cutters, became part of the U.S. Navy for the duration of World War I.

Saturday
7

1945—U.S. forces sank the Japanese battleship *Yamato* 200 miles north of Okinawa.

Sunday
8 EASTER SUNDAY

1961—The British passenger liner *Dara* exploded and sank in the Persian Gulf; 238 lives were lost.

TOM BOWLING

by Charles Disdain

Here, a sheer hulk, lies poor Tom Bowling,
The darling of our crew;
No more he'll hear the tempest howling,
For death has broached him to.
His form was of the manliest beauty,
His heart was kind and soft;
Faithful below, he did his duty,
And now he's gone aloft.

Tom never from his word departed,
His virtues were so rare,
His friends were many, and true-hearted,
His Poll was kind and fair:
And then he'd sing so blithe and jolly,
Ha, mane's the time and oft!
But mirth is turned to melancholy,
For Tom is gone aloft.

Yet shall poor Tom find pleasant weather,
When He, who all commands,
Shall give, to call life's crew together,
The word to pipe all hands.
Thus Death, who kings and tars dispatches,
In vain Tom's life has doff'd,
For, though his body's under hatches,
His soul is gone aloft.

If an old salt lay at death's door, his family and friends watched the tide. If he survived an ebb he would improve with the flood; he would always die on the ebb. —Samuel Eliot Morison

[Tides] are a real blessing, providing we know how to use them and are not irrational beings.... Let us carefully work the tides. They are constant, they are forcible, they are docile, if only we will take the trouble to understand them.

—Frank Cowper

FUNERAL NOTICE FOR A SAILOR, SALEM, MASSACHUSETTS, APRIL 14, 1798

Tom Bowling, another Sailor was buried this day. Tom kept it up till the last breath, swearing, raving, praying and the last came in only by the edges. He was a true Sailor, lost one hand in the American service, knew a ship well, and had all the true manners of a Ship of War. The song, Tom Bowling, was sung in private houses by his friends, and what his true name was I never could learn.

—Dr. William Bentley, clergyman

THE SUN, THE MOON, AND THE TIDES, ACCORDING TO F. W. STERLING

The range of a tide is the difference in height between high and low water. At new and full moon the sun and moon produce high tides at the same times. The effect of the sun augments that of the moon and the resultant high tides are higher than the average. Similarly the low tides are lower than the average, and the range of tides is greater. Tides at this season are called spring tides. At the time of first and third quarters of the moon the high tides due to the moon occur simultaneously with the low tides due to the sun. The resultant high and low tides are less than the average and the range is at its minimum. Tides occurring at this season are called neap tides. Tidal currents (flood and ebb) are strongest at spring tides and weakest at neap tides.

Low tide

High tide

A rising tide lifts all boats.
—old saying

APRIL

Monday
9 EASTER MONDAY / UK & CANADA

1925—William Beebe, who would set deep-sea diving records in his bathysphere, began his first undersea explorations in a homemade diving helmet.

Tuesday ◑
10

1858—Warren W. Shepard, marine artist, was born in Greenwich, New Jersey.

Wednesday
11

1922—The Gloucester fishing schooner *Henry Ford*, which lost the third International Fishermen's Race to Nova Scotia's *Bluenose*, was launched in Essex, Massachusetts

Thursday
12

1908—The American compromise sloop *Shadow*, one of the preeminent racing yachts of the era, was destroyed during a major fire that overwhelmed Chelsea, Massachusetts.

Friday
13

1926—Heavy seas from a northeast storm undermined and destroyed the decommissioned light tower at Cape Henlopen, Delaware.

Saturday
14

1740—Vice Admiral Edward "Old Grog" Vernon of the Royal Navy ordered that the daily rum ration be diluted with water.

Sunday
15

1851—The extreme clipper *Flying Cloud*, designed and built by Donald McKay, was launched in East Boston, Massachusetts.

So forth they rowed, and that Ferryman
With his stiff oares did brush the sea so strong,
That the hoare waters from his frigot ran,
And the light bubbles danced all along.
—Edmund Spenser

THE CONFEDERATE BLOCKADE RUNNER *FLORIDA*, ATLANTIC OCEAN EAST OF BAHAMAS, APRIL 20, 1864

At 6:25 p.m. made two sail. At 8 p.m. passed close across the bows of stranger, which we at first made abeam. Full-rigged brig, standing to the northward and westward. At 8:30 steam reported ready. At 8:40 backed main topsail and lowered screw. Remained hove to to let second chase come up. At 9:15 discovered that second chase was running well off and would cross us astern. Brailed up main trysail and gave chase with steam and sail, captain conning the ship. At 10 spoke the chase *Arial* ordered her to heave to. Sent third cutter aboard in charge of Lieutenant Barron. Stranger turned out as follows: Hermaphrodite brig *Mary*, Barbados, forty-three days out from Rio Grande, bound to New York; English register. At 10:50 hoisted boat and filled away.

—Lieutenant C. M. Morris, C. S. Navy

OARS VS. ENGINES, ACCORDING TO JOE COOMER

Oars rarely take you so far from home that you can't return with them. Oars cost thirty dollars a pair, an engine anywhere from eight hundred to five grand, and then it's useless until you feed it dollar bills in the form of gallons of gas.

ROWING IN ROUGH WATER

Wear a life jacket.

Relax; don't fight the water, work with it, try to become one with the motion of the boat.

Remain alert; keep an eye out for wind shifts, larger than average waves, shallows with breaking waves, etc.

Keep a light touch on the oars.

Use a short stroke.

On the recovery lift the blades high enough to clear the wave tops but not so high as to create excess windage.

When going into it, move your weight forward, which will allow the stern to weathercock.

When going with it, move your weight aft, which will allow the bow to weathercock.

But oars alone can ne'er prevail
To reach the distant coast;
The breath of heaven must swell the sail,
Or all the toil is lost.
—William Cowper

He looks one way and rows another.
—anon.

APRIL

Monday
16

1971—John Fairfax and Sylvia Cook embarked from San Francisco, California, on a voyage across the Pacific Ocean to Australia by oar in the 35-foot pulling boat *Britannia II.*

Tuesday ●
17

1962—*Miss U.S.A.*, driven by Roy Duby, broke the 200-mph barrier and set a world propeller-driven water-speed record to date of 200.419 mph, on Lake Guntersville, Alabama.

Wednesday
18

2002—Thor Heyerdahl, famous for sailing the raft *Kon-Tiki* from South America across the Pacific Ocean to the Tuamotu Islands, died in Colla Micheri, Italy.

Thursday
19

1850—The Clayton-Bulwer Treaty between the U.S. and Britain, which called for joint ownership of a proposed ship canal across Central America, was signed.

Friday
20

1938—Commander Robert D. Graham departed Bantry Bay, Ireland, in the 35-foot yawl *Caplin* on a voyage to the West Indies via Bermuda for which he would be awarded the Blue Water Medal of the Cruising Club of America.

Saturday
21

1971—Anders Svedlund departed Kalbarre, Western Australia, in the rowboat *Roslagen* on what would become the first solo crossing of the Indian Ocean under oars.

Sunday
22

1972—John Fairfax and Sylvia Cook arrived at Hayman Island, Australia, after crossing the Pacific Ocean from San Francisco in the rowboat *Britannia II.*

DINING SUPPLIES, LINER *OCEANIC*, AT THE APOGEE OF THE TRANSATLANTIC PASSENGER TRADE BETWEEN THE WORLD WARS

First- and second-class china—10,000 pieces
Third-class plates and cups—5,000 pieces
Breakage in a single voyage—800 to 1,000 plates
Glassware—4,500 pieces
Knives—3,600
Forks—5,200
Spoons—5,700
Tablecloths—1,000
Napkins—15,000
Napkin rings—700
Towels—15,000

The old-time ships were dull, plain, graceless, gloomy, and horribly depressing. They compelled the blues; one could not escape the blues in them. The modern idea is right: to surround the passenger with conveniences, luxuries, and abundance of inspiriting color.

—Mark Twain

THE OCEAN LINERS GET BIGGER AND BIGGER

Great Western, 1838—212 feet, 1,340 gross tons
Great Britain, 1845—322 feet, 3,270 gross tons
Great Eastern, 1860—689 feet, 18,915 gross tons
Mauretania, 1907—790 feet, 31,938 gross tons
Olympic, 1911—883 feet, 45,324 gross tons
Majestic, 1922—956 feet, 56,551 gross tons
Normandie, 1935—1,028 feet, 79,280 gross tons
France, 1962—1,035 feet, 66,348 gross tons
Voyager of the Seas, 1999—1,019 feet, 137,276 gross tons
Queen Mary 2, 2004—1,132 feet, 150,000 gross tons
Freedom of the Seas, 2005—1,112 feet, 158,000 gross tons

THE THREE CLASSES OF CREW MESSES ABOARD TRANSATLANTIC PASSENGER LINERS, LATE 19TH CENTURY (1, HIGHEST; 3, LOWEST)

1. Seamen, quartermasters, carpenters, etc.
2. Lamp-trimmers, servants, cooks, etc.
3. Engineroom stokers, greasers, and trimmers

THE OYSTER SLOOP *SPRAY*, GLOUCESTER HARBOR, MASSACHUSETTS, APRIL 24, 1895

The bay was feather-white as my little vessel tore in, smothered in foam. It was my first experience of coming into port alone, with a craft of any size, and in among shipping. Old fishermen ran down to the wharf for which the *Spray* was heading, apparently intent upon braining herself there. I hardly know how a calamity was averted, but with my heart in my mouth, almost, I let go the wheel, stepped quickly forward, and downed the jib. The sloop naturally rounded in the wind, and just ranging ahead, laid her cheek against a mooring-pile at the windward corner of the wharf, so quietly, after all, that she would not have broken an egg. Very leisurely I passed a rope around the post, and she was moored. Then a cheer went up from the little crowd on the wharf.

—Joshua Slocum

A ship is a noble thing.
—John Ruskin

APRIL

Monday
23

1997—*Titanic: The Musical* opened on Broadway, New York City.

Tuesday ◐
24

1988—The U.S. submarine *Bonefish*, off the coast of Florida, was severely damaged by a battery fire and explosion; three lives were lost.

Wednesday
25

1900—The Marconi International Marine Communication Company, specializing in wireless telegraphy, was founded.

Thursday
26

1898—The luxury passenger liner *New York* of the American Line, converted for combat in the Spanish-American War, was commissioned in the U.S. Navy as the USS *Harvard*.

Friday
27

1863—The British mail steamer *Anglo-Saxon* struck a reef off Cape Race, Newfoundland; 237 of 446 people on board perished.

Saturday
28

1865—Sir Samuel Cunard, founder of the Cunard Line, died in England.

Sunday
29

1862—Union naval forces under Admiral David Farragut, U.S. Navy, captured the city of New Orleans.

For every fifty who go on long ocean cruises, there are 50,000 who go on short ones.

—W. E. Warrington

THE 46-FOOT SLOOP-YACHT *ISOLT*, OFF BERMUDA, MAY 5, 1906

Whole mainsail, staysail and jib set; light Easterly air all day. We eat our stew with relish. The ice gives out. The useless cook has not pumped the melted water out of the ice refrigerator. I swear I will kill him and also kill Williams [the paid hand], but recant and let them live. Now they both want to eat our own cooked grub! Shocking! What shall we do with them? Reefed mainsail. 7 P.M.—S.E. strong winds, on port tack, heading about S. by E., with very rough seas. Sighted Gibbs Hill Light of Bermuda, bearing S.E. 20 miles. At 11 P.M. tacked ship; wind East, heading N.E. by N. to clear the Northern Bermuda reefs, about two points free. The *Isolt* fairly jumps along by the wind, under reefed mainsail, staysail and jib. Weather shut in very thick; lost sight of Gibbs Hill Light; blowing hard, and a wretched cross sea running over our fore deck and washing all things well. Not much sleep this night; watching and anxious to get in and avoid the reefs near the S.S. *Madiana* wreck. We see nothing but silver foam and fiery seas capped with darkness, not a star in sight.

—W. E. Meyer

THE CRUISING BOAT, ACCORDING TO ARTHUR STURGES HILDEBRAND

Cruising, you are at once a wanderer, and a stay-at-home; you carry your house with you everywhere, and it carries you. It is the best of houses—a snug, trim habitation, weather-tight, sheltered and secluded, although the weather itself, wind, rain, and sea, is just outside. It is compact and complete—large enough, yet not too large—neatly kept, since there is no room to have it otherwise, convenient, since disorder and a ship do not agree, resourceful, since you are cut off from all the world. To live aboard a ship is the best of lives.

A NOMAD OF THE SEA

The cruiser has the great advantage over the tourist, the cyclist, or the pedestrian—he is independent of all hotels, and carries all his comforts with him. He has the constant luxury of a well-ordered home, an ample wardrobe, a well-stocked table, a cosy bed. Unlike the traveller in caravans, he has no cattle to look after, no prying villagers to distract him, no petty annoyances to put up with. Free and untrammelled as the winds, reckless as a viking, adventurous as a Columbus, he roams wherever the wind and his fancy lead him, with the carelessness of a vagabond and the home comforts of domestic life. A veritable nomad of the summer sea.

—Frank Cowper

However short the voyage we never lose all the shine of it.
—H. M. Tomlinson

APRIL/MAY

Monday
30

1943—The submarine HMS *Seraph*, off the coast of Spain, dropped overboard a dead man dressed as a British military intelligence officer and planted with false invasion plans to confuse the Germans about the when and where of D-day.

Tuesday
1

1897—A conference was called at the Fifth Avenue Hotel in New York City to take the first serious steps toward the establishment of the North American Yacht Racing Union.

Wednesday ○
2

1969—The ocean liner *Queen Elizabeth 2* got underway from England on her maiden transatlantic passage to New York.

Thursday
3

1802—A marine hospital for sick and disabled seamen was established in New Orleans, Louisiana, by an Act of Congress.

Friday
4

1493—Pope Alexander VI issued the Bull of Demarcation, which provided that all discoveries westward of a meridian 100 leagues west of the Azores belonged to Spain, and all eastward of it belonged to Portugal.

Saturday
5

1768—Thomas Buttersworth, marine artist, was born on the Isle of Wight, England.

Sunday
6

1994—Queen Elizabeth II and President François Mitterrand officially opened the Chunnel, the Channel Tunnel linking England and France.

DAMAGE CONTROL KIT FOR CRUISING BOATS

Softwood wedges
Softwood plugs of a diameter that fits all the seacocks
Nylon wire ties
Hatchet or small fireman's-style ax
Sledgehammer
Mallet—wooden or hard rubber
Screwdrivers, slotted and Phillips-head
Fast-cutting saw
Bolt cutters
Stillson wrench
Stainless-steel hose clamps, various sizes, plus several that fit all the hose and pipe diameters on board
Rubber inner-tube material
Oakum, at least a pound
Duct tape
Pieces of hose, various lengths and diameters
Split fire hose, several pieces
Marline or twine, several balls
Rags

EMERGENCY KIT FOR THE DINGHY, IN THE EVENT YOU HAVE TO TAKE TO IT IN A HURRY

Bailer and hand pump
Spare oarlocks, or thole pins and grommets
Spare oars
Hatchet or small ax
Anchor and rode
Life jackets and cushions
Flashlight, matches, spare batteries, compass, binoculars, signaling devices
Food and fresh water

THE SAILING PACKET *CAROLINE*, ST. LAWRENCE RIVER, CANADA, BELOW QUEBEC CITY, MAY 10, 1834

We cast anchor again at eleven o'clock last night, but got under weigh about 2 a.m. to take advantage of the tide which runs very rapidly at about 6 knots. I believe it never runs more than 3½ knots in the Thames. The river is the most dangerous part of our voyage. We have already passed two wrecked vessels, one three days ago, and the other this morning called the *Cherub* from Greenock. It is jammed in amongst the rocks, and was wrecked on one of the dark nights at the beginning of the week, probably on Tuesday. The winds in the river are particularly changeable. You may see at the same moment one vessel carrying along on a fair wind, another becalmed and a third with it directly ahead; this is caused by the high mountains on each side. There are also many small islands, some are nothing more than rocks, others are covered with brushwood. We passed one yesterday called Hare Island with numerous hares upon it from which it derives its name. All the way on our larboard side are houses, but to starboard are very high hills with their summits covered with snow.

—C. H. Clarke

Of all things the ship is the most cosmopolitan.
—L. G. Carr Laughton

MAY

Monday
7 BANK HOLIDAY / UK

1971—The *Emma C. Berry*, a Noank smack built in 1866, now on exhibit at Mystic Seaport in Connecticut, was relaunched after restoration.

Tuesday
8

1991—The *Longshot*, a hydrofoil trimaran skippered by Russell Long, set a world speed record under sail to date of 38.13 knots on a half-kilometer (500-meter) course in Bodega Bay, California.

Wednesday
9

1926—Richard Byrd and Floyd Bennett of the U.S. Navy made the first flight by an airplane over the North Pole.

Thursday ◑
10

1946—W. P. (William Picard) Stephens, boatbuilder, designer, author of *Traditions and Memories of American Yachting*, and *Canoe and Boatbuilding for Amateurs*, among other works, died in Bayside, New York.

Friday
11

1962—The Columbia River Maritime Museum was established in Astoria, Washington.

Saturday
12

563—St. Columba landed on the island of Iona, Inner Hebrides, Scotland, at the end of a passage from Ireland in an open, skin-covered currach.

Sunday
13 MOTHER'S DAY / US & CANADA

1923—The medium clipper *Glory of the Seas*, the last clipper ship built by Donald McKay, was burned on a beach near Seattle, Washington.

EXTRAORDINARY FEATS OF THE SAILOR

Shellback—a sailor who has joined the Order of the Shellback by crossing the equator by sea

Shellback of the Golden Dragon—a sailor who has entered the Domain of the Golden Dragon by crossing the International Date Line by sea

Golden Shellback—a sailor who has crossed the International Date Line and the equator at the same time

Mossback—a sailor who has sailed around Cape Horn

Horned Shellback—a sailor who has rounded Cape Horn and crossed the equator on the same voyage

Blue Nose—a sailor who has entered the Northern Domain of the Polar Bear by crossing the Arctic Circle by sea

Frozen Stiff—a sailor who has entered the Royal Domain of the Emperor Penguin by crossing the Antarctic Circle by sea

To say the truth, from what I have observed in the behaviour of sailors...I am convinced that on land there is nothing more idle and dissolute; in their own element, there are no persons near the level of their degree.

—Henry Fielding

It has mistakenly been suggested that mariners are barbarous and incapable of leading more sensible and refined lives.

—Georges Fournier

Sailors, with their built-in sense of order, service, and discipline, should really be running the world.

—Nicholas Monsarrat

THE FOUR-MASTED COASTING SCHOONER *ALBERT F. PAUL*, OFF GEORGETOWN, SOUTH CAROLINA, MAY 18, 1933

Fresh breeze but moderating, called all hands at 5 A.M. Coffee. Hove in some chain. Put a harbor furl on the jibs. Sea going down. The tugboat *W. H. Andrews* came out about 10 A.M. The pilot, Captain Porter, came aboard. Passed the hawser to the tugboat, hove in the anchor, and got under weigh. Set the main, mizzen, and forestaysail. The tug could not keep ahead of the vessel. Hauled down the forestaysail and dropped the peak of the mizzen. Fifteen miles up Winyah Bay to Georgetown. About two miles below the town lowered the main and mizzen sails and tied them up. Unhooked the jib sheets and coiled then down close up in the bow to be out of the way. Unshackled the lower fore, main, and mizzen sheet blocks, pulled them up two blocks, and coiled the sheets over the ends of the booms. Hove the main and mizzen booms up well clear of the deck to be out of the way when loading. Put shores under the boom jaws and unhooked the throat halliards which will be used in loading. When the vessel was abreast the town the tug blew three long blasts of the whistle to let the townspeople know a vessel had arrived in town.

—James S. McCullough

The sailor out of water is, indeed, as wretched an animal as the fish out of water.
—Henry Fielding

MAY

Monday
14

1927—The Chesapeake and Delaware Canal, connecting the Delaware River and Chesapeake Bay, was officially reopened after being deepened to 12 feet and widened to 150 feet.

Tuesday
15

1928—Walt Disney's Mickey Mouse made his first film appearance, in the cartoon *Steamboat Willy*.

Wednesday ●
16

1966—Merchant seamen went on strike in Britain, crippling shipping; the dispute came to an end on July 1.

Thursday
17

1797—The great mutiny of sailors in the British fleet moored at Spithead, near Portsmouth, England, ended when the demands of the sailors were granted.

Friday
18

1901—The 141-foot Crowninshield-designed sloop *Independence*, planked below the waterline with bronze plates over steel frames, candidate for the defense of the America's Cup, was launched in Boston, Massachusetts.

Saturday
19

1918—Florence Chadwick, the first person to swim the English Channel in both directions, was born.

Sunday
20

1774—The British Parliament, to punish rebellious colonists, passed an act to close the port of Boston, Massachusetts.

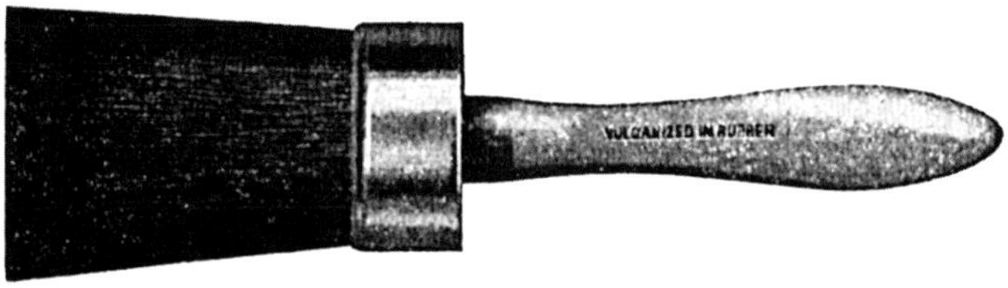

SCHEDULE FOR PAINTING A NEW BOAT

Prime coat outside
Prime coat inside
First coat bottom paint
Inside finish coats
Outside finish coats
Final coat bottom paint (just before launching)

Allow plenty of time between coats for proper drying.

TOPSIDES PAINT

Keep in mind that dark colors absorb the heat of the sun and light colors reflect it.

Hot climates—light colors
Cool climates—darker colors

Avoid black and very dark colors (dark green, navy blue, maroon, etc.) unless the boat will be used in cold climates.

DECK PAINT

To protect against the heat of the sun, use light colors—off-white, light gray, light yellow, buff, etc.

To make the deck nonskid, fill a salt shaker with fine sand and sprinkle the final coat while it is still wet.

HOMEMADE DECK OIL

1 part spar varnish
2 parts linseed oil
3 parts turpentine
1 teaspoon Japan drier

Apply over bare wood or previously oil-treated surface with a brush or rag. Allow to stand for 15 minutes, wipe off excess with dry rag, let dry. More coats equal more durability. Additional coats can be applied at any time; no sanding required—simply clean the original surface. Creates a low-maintenance, elastic, easily touched-up, inexpensive, varnishlike matte finish.

Note: Linseed-oil–based finishes tend to darken over time. To prevent this, use tung oil instead of linseed. (Tung oil, however, is more expensive.)

TO REDUCE THE TIME AND COST OF UPKEEP

Painted surfaces generally require only one new coat per year; varnished, two to three coats.

THE SHIP *ALERT*, PACIFIC OCEAN NEAR THE EQUATOR, MAY 22, 1836

This day it rained nearly all day, and...we stopped up the scuppers and filled the decks with rain water, and bringing all our clothes on deck, had a grand wash, fore and aft. When this was through, we stripped to our drawers, and taking pieces of soap and strips of canvas for towels, we turned-to and soaped, washed, and scrubbed one another down, to get off, as we said, the California dust; for the common wash in salt water, which is all Jack can get, being on an allowance of fresh, had little efficacy, and was more for taste than utility.... By unplugging the holes, we let the soap-suds off the decks, and in a short time had a new supply of rain water, in which we had a grand rinsing. It was surprising to see how much soap and fresh water did for the complexions of many of us; how much of what we supposed to be tan and sea-blacking, we got rid of.

—Richard Henry Dana, Jr.

Putty and paint
Make the devil a saint.
—anon.

MAY

Monday
21 VICTORIA DAY / CANADA

1846—A steamship docked in Honolulu, the first such vessel to visit Hawaii.

Tuesday
22

1933—National Maritime Day was first celebrated in the United States.

Wednesday ◐
23

1701—Captain William Kidd, convicted of piracy, was hanged at Execution Dock, Wapping, London, England.

Thursday
24

1950—Marcel Bardiaux departed Ouistreham, France, in the 30-foot home-built sloop *Les Quatre Vents* on a circumnavigation of the globe for which he would be awarded the Blue Water Medal of the Cruising Club of America.

Friday
25

1937—The Golden Gate Bridge, at the mouth of San Francisco Bay, California, was opened to traffic.

Saturday
26

1788—John Paul Jones, formerly of the Continental Navy, now a rear admiral in the Russian Navy, was given command of a Black Sea squadron.

Sunday
27

1907—Rachel Carson, author of *The Sea Around Us* and *Under the Sea-Wind*, was born in Springdale, Pennsylvania.

THE FIRST 25 YACHT CLUBS

Flotilla of the Neva, Russia, 1718
Water Club of the Harbor of Cork, Ireland, 1720
Cumberland Fleet (now the Royal Thames Yacht Club), England, 1775
The Yacht Club, England, 1815
Royal Yacht Club, England, 1820
Royal Northern Yacht Club, Ireland, 1824
Singapore Yacht Club, Singapore, 1824
Royal Western Yacht Club, England, 1827
Segelsallskapet, Sweden, 1830
Royal Irish Yacht Club, Ireland, 1831
Kungliga Svenska Segel Sallskapet, Sweden , 1832
Royal Swedish Yacht Club, Sweden, 1832
Royal Yacht Squadron, England, 1833
Royal London Yacht Club, England, 1833
Royal Eastern Yacht Club, England, 1835
Royal Nova Scotia Yacht Squadron, Canada, 1837
Royal Hobart Regatta Association, Tasmania, 1838
Royal Southern Yacht Club, England, 1838
Royal St. George Yacht Club, Ireland, 1838
Société des Régates du Havre, France, 1838
Detroit Boat Club, USA, 1839
Royal Perth Yacht Club, Australia, 1841
Royal Harwich Yacht Club, England, 1843
New York Yacht Club, New York, 1844
Royal Bermuda Yacht Club, Bermuda, 1844

Resolved that such members as shall talk of sailing after dinner to be fined a bumper.

—from the rules of the Water Club of the Harbor of Cork, Ireland, 1720

ELECTION OF MEMBERS, RULES AND REGULATIONS OF THE EASTERN YACHT CLUB, MARBLEHEAD, MASSACHUSETTS, 1914

No candidate for membership who is not a yacht owner shall be admitted while the Club has a total of seven hundred or more active members.

A woman owning a yacht may be elected a Flag Member, and shall pay annual dues, but no initiation fee. Such membership shall continue only during the period of yacht ownership and shall carry only the following privileges:

1. Of flying the Club flag.
2. Of registering private signal with the Secretary.
3. Of entering yacht in Club races.
4. Of using Club stations and floats.
5. Of using the Club House as prescribed for ladies.

THE PACKET SHIP *GARRICK*, MID-ATLANTIC OCEAN, JUNE 3, 1854

Wind east to S.E. 2 to 3 knots. A swell from the E.N.E., N.N.E. and westward. Appearances indicate a northerly wind. Mercury falling, swell increasing and atmosphere cooling. Surely we must have a change. 6 p.m., tacked to southward. Until 12 p.m. wind veered from east to S.E. by S. 12, tacked to northward and eastward. Wind veering to S.E. A rolling swell from E.S.E. and E.N.E. Weather pleasant. Course N. 59 E. Distance 61 miles. Threw over a well corked and copper wired bottle.

—Captain R. W. Foster

Yachtin' is a gintlemans' sport, an' in daling with gintlemen ye can't be too careful.
—"Mr. Dooley" [Finley Peter Dunne]

MAY/JUNE

Monday
28 MEMORIAL DAY / US
SPRING BANK HOLIDAY / UK

1892—The Seawanhaka Corinthian Yacht Club, founded in 1871, merged with the Oyster Bay Yacht Club and officially opened its new clubhouse on Centre Island, Oyster Bay, New York.

Tuesday
29

1630—King Charles II, generally credited with the introduction of the sport of yachting to England, was born in London.

Wednesday
30

1946—Winfield M. [Martin] Thompson, yachtsman, journalist, author of *The Lawson History of the America's Cup*, frequent contributor to *The Rudder* magazine in its early years, died in California.

Thursday
31

1997—The Confederation Bridge, linking Prince Edward Island with New Brunswick, opened to regular traffic.

Friday ○
1

1815—The Yacht Club, later the Royal Yacht Club, the first of its type in England, was established during a meeting at the Thatched House Tavern, St. James's Street, London.

Saturday
2

1877—Officers of the British royal yacht *Osborne* sighted a sea serpent off the coast of Sicily.

Sunday
3

1969—The Australian aircraft carrier HMAS *Melbourne* collided with the American destroyer USS *Frank E. Evans* and cut it in half off the coast of South Vietnam.

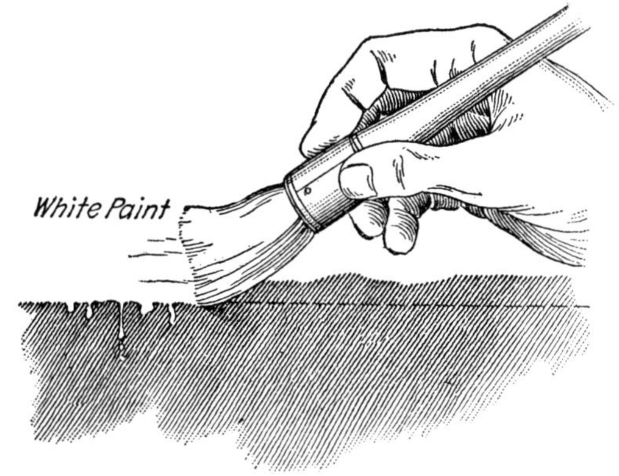

THE BASIC TYPES OF MODERN COPPER ANTIFOULING PAINT

Rosin—soft, low abrasion resistance, moderate antifouling protection; good for slow-speed craft in northern climates; least expensive type

Resin, or resin-rosin combination—semi-hard, moderate abrasion resistance, moderate antifouling protection; good for average boats with average use; moderately expensive

Vinyl—hard, tough, smooth finish, with moderate antifouling protection; ideal for racing craft; expensive

Epoxy—hard, tough, very abrasion-resistant, moderate antifouling protection; good for boats launched from trailers or on and off a beach; expensive

Copolymer—moderately hard, good abrasion resistance, good antifouling protection; good protection for craft that see hard use in warmer climates; expensive

Water-based—moderately hard, low abrasion resistance, moderate antifouling protection; less disagreeable to apply because of lack of chemical solvents; moderately expensive

THE TWO PURPOSES OF ANTIFOULING BOTTOM PAINT

1. Protection against worms
2. Protection against weed

Depending on where the boat will be used, some bottom paints are better than others. Ask around to determine which is best for your location.

TO ESTIMATE THE AMOUNT OF BOTTOM PAINT REQUIRED

Determine the square footage of the hull bottom and compare with the coverage per square foot posted on the label of the can

Powerboat or shallow-draft sailboat with long keel: A = LWL x (B+D)

Modern fin-keel racer-cruiser with spade rudder: A = LWL x (B+D) x .5

Traditional deep-keel displacement sailboat: A = LWL x (B+D) x .75

A = area
LWL = waterline length
B = beam at the waterline
D = draft

THE WOOL CLIPPER *ORIENT*, SOUTH ATLANTIC OCEAN, JULY 10, 1862

I witnessed a splendid sunrise at 7 a.m. It is a fine morning, but a dead calm. There is a ship in sight over the stern, in the same predicament as ourselves, becalmed. 11 a.m. A breeze sprang up and sent us flying along; the ship in our wake tried hard to catch us so the captain took in sail and waited for her to see if she wanted anything. She proved to be the *Tyburnia* from London to Bombay, sailing six days before us; she signalled for a supply of flour, but as we were on short allowance we could not spare any. The two captains signalled to each other for more than an hour, and arranged to keep company during the night and burn blue lights occasionally as we were close on the South American coast off St Salvador. Yesterday we were off Rio San Francisco. The *Tyburnia* reports herself 43 days out, all well.

—Edward Lacey

Every day brings a ship,
Every ship brings a word.
—Ralph Waldo Emerson

JUNE

Monday
4

1849—The Pacific Mail Steamship Company began a regular run between the Isthmus of Panama and San Francisco, carrying forty-niners and mining equipment out and returning with gold from the minefields.

Tuesday
5

1972—Solidarity, a Polish shipyard labor union, winning a freely contested election, became the first opposition party in the Communist bloc to defeat the Communist Party,

Wednesday
6

1850—A San Francisco newspaper reported 509 vessels at anchor off the city, most of which had brought forty-niners to California in the search for gold.

Thursday
7

1978—Naomi James, originally from New Zealand, returned to England in the 53-foot cutter *Express Crusader*, thus becoming the first woman to sail around the world alone.

Friday ◑
8

1813—Admiral David Dixon Porter, U.S. Navy, hero of the American Civil War, was born in Chester, Pennsylvania.

Saturday
9

1534—An exploring expedition led by Jacques Cartier discovered the St. Lawrence River.

Sunday
10

1854—The first graduation exercises were held at the U.S. Naval Academy, Annapolis, Maryland.

EARLY EPIC SMALL-BOAT ADVENTURES, A FEW OF THE MOST NOTABLE

1789—Captain William Bligh and 18 loyalists from the mutiny on HMS *Bounty* survived a seven-week, 3,600-mile voyage in an open ship's boat in the Pacific Ocean.

1870—J. C. Buckley and Nicholas Primoraz made the first east-to-west crossing of the Atlantic Ocean in a small sailboat, the *City of Ragua*, from Cork, Ireland, to Boston, Massachusetts.

1875—Nathaniel Bishop rowed the 12-foot sneakbox *Centennial Republic* down the Ohio and Mississippi Rivers from Pittsburgh, Pennsylvania, to the Gulf of Mexico.

1876—The Banks fisherman Alfred Johnson sailed the 20-foot dory *Centennial* across the Atlantic Ocean, the first singlehanded west-to-east passage.

1877—Thomas Crapo and his wife, Joanna, sailed a dory across the Atlantic Ocean from New Bedford, Massachusetts, to Penzance, England.

1880–81—Frederick Norman and George P. Thomas made the first double crossing under sail of the Atlantic Ocean, from Gloucester, Massachusetts, to Cowes, Isle of Wight, England, and back again.

1891—In a west-to-east race under sail across the Atlantic Ocean against William Andrews, Josiah Lawlor managed to hold on and win in the 15-foot *Sea Serpent*, despite capsizing several times during stormy weather.

1892—William Albert Andrews set a record for the smallest boat to cross the Atlantic Ocean in the 14½-foot *Sapolio;* the record would stand for 73 years.

1896—George Harbo and Frank Samuelson became the first to row across the Atlantic Ocean, in the 18-foot *Fox*, from New York City to the Scilly Isles, England.

THE WORST PART CAN BE THE BEST PART, ACCORDING TO JACK LONDON

The mishaps are almost the best part of small-boat sailing. Looking back, they prove to be punctuations of joy. At the time they try your mettle and your vocabulary, and may make you so pessimistic as to believe that God has a grudge against you—but afterward, ah, afterward, with what pleasure you remember them and with what gusto do you relate them to your brother skippers in the fellowhood of small-boat sailing!

LAST LOG ENTRY, YAWL *PERSEUS*, ENGLISH CHANNEL, JUNE 12, 1891

Wind N.E., fresh and fine. 6 A.M., under way with mainsail only; very much work. Eventually got early tea. Set jib and mizen; washed, and prepared breakfast before reaching Dover. 9 to 10, hove-to in Dover Bay, had breakfast, &c., and sailed again. 10.30, set large jib. 11, off Folkestone, going grandly, but the wind soon fell light. 2.30 P.M., passed Dungeness against tide; wind E.S.E., light. 7 P.M., St. Leonards; wind S.S.W., light; boat making good way, owing to smoother water and the large jib. 8.30 P.M., anchored off Bexhill; night fine.

—R. T. McMullen

If you want to understand the sea, you've got to sail over it in a boat small enough to let you lean over the side and touch the Face of the Waters.
—Weston Martyr

JUNE

Monday 11

1764—Sandy Hook Light, New Jersey, at the southern entrance to New York Harbor, whose tower is the oldest original one still standing and in use in the United States, was illuminated for the first time.

Tuesday 12

1880—Frederick Norman and George P. Thomas got underway from Gloucester, Massachusetts, in the 16-foot cutter *Little Western* on the first leg of the first-ever double crossing under sail by small boat of the Atlantic Ocean (east to west, west to east).

Wednesday 13

1918—The Netherlands parliament passed an act calling for the damming of the Zuider Zee, the draining of various parts, and the creation of the Ijsselmeer.

Thursday 14 FLAG DAY

2003—The schooner *Fame*, a reproduction of a privateer from the War of 1812, was launched in Essex, Massachusetts.

Friday 15 ●

1891—French fishermen found the British singlehander R. T. McMullen, author of *Down Channel*, dead at the tiller of the yacht *Perseus*, bound for the last time down the English Channel.

Saturday 16

1903—An expedition led by Roald Amundsen got underway from Oslo, Norway, in the ship Gjoa on the first east–west transit of the Northwest Passage.

Sunday 17 FATHER'S DAY

1940—The Cunard Line's *Lancastria* was sunk by German bombers off St. Nazaire, France, while evacuating Allied soldiers and refugees; between 4,000 and 9,000 lives were lost.

THE MONKEY AT SEA

Monkey—a small, single-masted, square-rigged coasting vessel of the 16th and 17th centuries; a wooden container for carrying grog from the cask to the seamen's mess, British Royal Navy; a specialized steam engine; a weight used in a mechanical pile driver; a sailor who is agile in the rigging; a type of small cannon; a rack for storing cannon balls

Monkey boat—a type of small, narrow canal boat

Monkey dicks—sausages (slang)

Monkey gaff—a short gaff set above the spanker gaff

Monkey jacket—a close-fitting jacket worn by sailors

Monkey pump—a straw used to suck liquid from a hole in a cask

Monkey block—a small, single block with a swivel strop

Monkey island—the upper bridge on a ship's superstructure

Monkey bridge—a narrow fore-and-aft bridge on a sailing ship connecting the poop to the forecastle deck

Monkey march—U.S. Marine Corps slang for a close-order march

Monkey wrench—a type of wrench used by the ship's black gang

Monkey face—a triangular metal plate with holes in the corners; used for shackling the ends of three chains

Monkey fist—a heavy knot at the end of a heaving line

Monkey forecastle—a small, elevated forecastle or anchor deck

Monkey foresail—square foresail set flying on a fore-and-aft–rigged vessel

Monkey on a stick—skewered chicken (slang)

Monkey poop—a low house on a raised quarterdeck

Monkey rail—a rail above the quarter rail on a sailing vessel

Monkey rope—a rope tied around a sailor's waist for security when working over the side

Monkey shit—packing material for stuffing boxes (slang)

Monkey spar—a spar smaller than the one usually used for the purpose

Monkey tail—rudder horn; a short hand spike

Powder monkey—a boy who carried gunpowder from the magazine to the gun crews

A Yankee sloop came down the river,
Hah, hah, rolling John,
Oh, what do you think that sloop had in her?
Hah, hah, rolling John,
Monkey's hide and bullock's liver,
Hah, hah, rolling John.

—old anchor chantey

HIS MAJESTY'S PACKET *LADY HOBART*, ON THE GRAND BANK, NEWFOUNDLAND, JUNE 22, 1803

Cape Race bearing NNW ½ W 123 miles distant, discovered a large schooner under French colours, standing towards us, with her deck full of men. From her manner of bearing down upon us, we concluded she had been apprized of the war, and that she took us for a merchant brig. Cleared ship for action. At eight being within range of our guns, fired a shot at her, when she struck her colours. Sent on board and took possession of the vessel; she proved to be *l'Aimable Julie*, of Port Liberty, of eighty tons burden, strong built, bound thither from the island of St. Pierre, laden with salt-fish, and commanded by Citizen Charles Roffe. —William Dorset Fellowes

There is a witchery in the sea.
—Richard Henry Dana, Jr.

JUNE

Monday
18

1856—From the log of the clipper ship *James Baines*, several hundred miles west of Cape Horn, at 8:30 p.m.: "In all starboard stud sails, ship going 21 knots with main skysail set."

Tuesday
19

1941—President Franklin Roosevelt, in anticipation of a naval war in both the Atlantic and the Pacific Oceans at the same time, signed the Two Ocean Navy Expansion Act.

Wednesday
20

1925—The U.S. Coast Guard used an aircraft for the first time to chase rumrunners.

Thursday
21

SUMMER SOLSTICE

1873—H. M. (Henry Major) Tomlinson, author of *The Sea and the Jungle*, *Gallions Reach*, *London River*, and other literature of the sea, was born in Poplar, London, England.

Friday ◐
22

1844—For the first time, a keelless racing rowing craft—ancestor to the modern racing shell—*The Five Brothers*, built by Harry Clasper and rowed by the five Clasper brothers, took first place at the Royal Thames Regatta, England.

Saturday
23

1626—A large codfish opened up at Cambridge Market, England, was found to contain a copy of a book of religious treatises by John Frith.

Sunday
24

1904—The Danish passenger liner *Norge* ran ashore on Rockall Island northwest of Ireland and sank; of 780 aboard, 550 were lost.

THE SAINTLY FIGUREHEAD

There was an ancient carver that carved of a
saint,
But the parson wouldn't have it, so he took a
pot of paint
And changed its angel garments for a
dashing soldier rig,
And said it was a figurehead and sold
it to a brig.

The brig hauled her mainsail to an off shore
draft,
Then she shook her snowy royals and the Scil-
lies went abaft;
And cloudy with her canvas she ran before the
Trade
Till she got to the Equator, where she struck a
merrymaid.

A string of pearls and conches were all the
mermaid's togs,
But the flying-fish and porpoises—they followed
her like dogs;
She had a voice of silver and lips of coral red,
She climbed the dolphin-striker and kissed
the figurehead.

And every starry evening in the Doldrum calms
She'd wriggle up the bobstay and throw her
tender arms
About his scarlet shoulders and fondle him
and cry
And stroke his curly whiskers, but he never
winked an eye.

Songs o'love she sings him, the livelong day,
And she hangs upon his bosom and sobs the
night away,
But he never, never answers, for beneath his
soldier paint
The wooden-headed lunatic still thinks that
he's a saint.

—from "The Figurehead, a Salt Sea Yarn,"
by Crosbie Garstin

THE SAME BY A DIFFERENT NAME

England—mermaid
Cornwall—merrymaid
Ireland—merrow, or muirruhgach
Isle of Man—ben-varry
Shetland Islands—sea-trow
Scandinavia—neck; havmand; havfine
Germany—meerfrau
Russia—rusalka
Spain—sirena

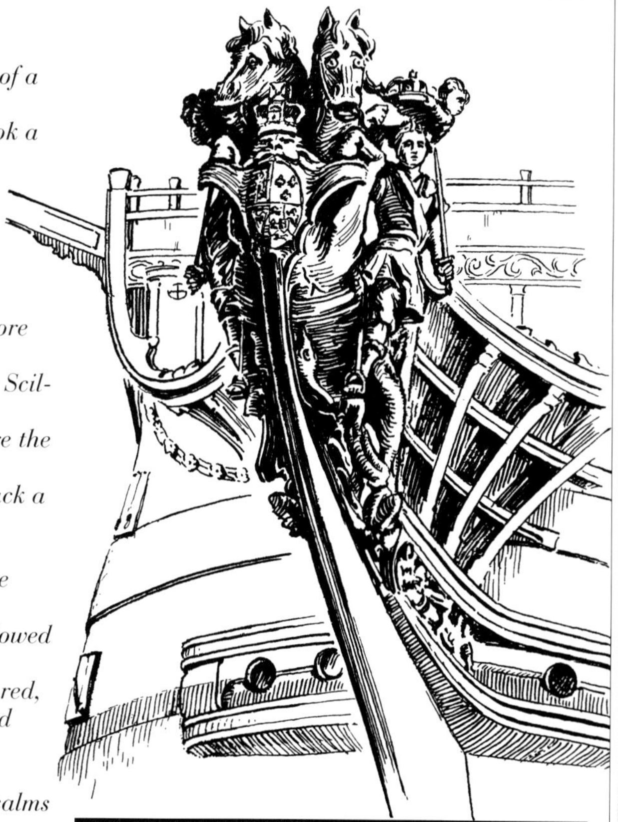

THE 13 ½-FOOT SLOOP *TINKERBELLE*, TRANSATLANTIC PASSAGE, JUNE 30, 1965

The last day of June and I'm only about one-third of the way. I don't think the rest of the trip will take two months, but I think it will take me until Aug. 15, all right. I was becalmed for a couple of hours. Lay out on deck and snoozed a bit. When I looked around again the ocean seemed full of dolphins, in widely separated groups. I wonder how those far in the rear kept from getting lost. Later in the afternoon *Tinkerbelle* was visited by some very colorful fish, three or four feet long, with dark iridescent blue bodies, two forward fins of lighter blue, and bright yellow tails. They cruised back and forth under the boat as I was having supper and wouldn't take any of the juicy morsels I offered them. Sailing in the dark, later, I was "pursued" by a couple of thunderstorms. Lightning flashes lit up the entire sky, although they were too far off for me to hear the thunder. Finally, at about 1:30 A.M. *(Tinkerbelle* time), I decided to bed down and, wouldn't you know it, that's when the first ship I've seen in days appeared. Fortunately it passed well to the south.

—Robert Manry

At first there was only the calm endlessness of the evening sea....
—Thomas Wolfe

JUNE/JULY

Monday 25

1861—The Cunard Line's luxury transatlantic passenger steamer *Scotia*—first-class accommodations only—winner of the Blue Riband, was launched in Glasgow, Scotland.

Tuesday 26

1884—Congress authorized the commissioning of graduates of the Naval Academy as ensigns in the U.S. Navy.

Wednesday 27

1871—William Curtis, a founder of the New York Athletic Club, received a patent for a much-improved rowing machine for off-the-water training of oarsmen.

Thursday 28

1932—Yacht designer John Alden became the first skipper to win the Bermuda Race three times—1923, in *Malabar IV*; 1926, in *Malabar VII*; and 1932, in *Malabar X*.

Friday 29

1952—The USS *Oriskany* became the first aircraft carrier to round Cape Horn.

Saturday 30

1853—The clipper ship *Matchless*, built for the California trade, was launched in Chelsea, Massachusetts.

Sunday 1

1879—The U.S. Lifeboat Station at Buffalo, New York, was established.

RETRIEVING THE ANCHOR, ACCORDING TO DIXON KEMP

If an anchor is let go on very firm holding-ground, or on ground where the anchor is likely to get foul, a tripping line is made fast to the crown of the anchor; to the other end of the line a buoy is made fast, and when the anchor is "wanted" it can be broken out of the ground by hauling on the tripping line if it cannot be got by hauling on the cable.

Another plan is to "scow" the anchor by bending the end of the cable to the crown instead of to the ring or shackle. The cable is then "stopped" to the ring by a yarn. When the cable is hauled upon the stop breaks, and, of course, the cable being fast to the crown, the anchor is readily broken out of the ground. A boat should not be left moored with her anchor "scowed," as, if any unusual strain came upon the cable, the stop would break, and the boat would probably go adrift. The trip line should be used in such cases.

ANCHOR TERMS

Bite—the anchor has taken a good hold in the ground

Acockbill—the anchor is hanging by its chain over the bow

Apeak—the anchor line has been hove short and the anchor is about to break free from the ground

Coming home—the anchor begins to drag

Bring home—pull the vessel up to the anchor

Up and down—the anchor chain is vertical, the anchor is about to break out of the ground

Breaks ground—the anchor has broken out of its bed on the bottom

Shod—the anchor has broken out of the ground and has thus lost its maximum holding strength

Aweigh—the anchor is off the bottom

Atrip—the anchor has broken free of the ground

Cat—haul the ring of the anchor to the cathead (a heavy timber projecting from the bow)

Club—ride with the current while the anchor is dragging

Fish—bring the flukes of an anchor to the rail after it has been hauled to the cathead

THE 20-FOOT KNOCKABOUT *VIVIAN*, GULF COAST OF FLORIDA, JULY 4, 1898

We sailed up the bay to Englewood, about four miles, by a most tortuous channel and had centerboard drill, as that article made constant acquaintance with all the bars en route, and often with the bottom of the channel. This town is supposed to be somewhere, but it isn't; we found only a forgotten Winter hotel, one store, an old sawmill, and three or four houses well scattered. At the sawmill we met a man thoroughly saturated with local color. He was a Southern salt, and his language was, to say the least, picturesque; it would have done credit to a pirate.... I must just mention the mosquitoes down there. At dusk they came aboard as a cloud settles on a mountain peak. But our nettings kept them out, and the large windows gave us the benefit of the light night airs, keeping the cabin right cool.

—J. Foster Searles

The single commandment of anchoring is "Thou shalt create scope."
—Reese Palley

JULY

Monday
2
CANADA DAY

1912—The *Detroit*, the first small motorboat to cross the Atlantic Ocean, got underway from Detroit, Michigan, on the first leg of her epic voyage.

Tuesday
3

1998—The *Cable & Wireless Adventurer* set a record to date for the fastest circumnavigation of the globe by a power vessel: 74 days, 20 hours, 58 minutes, 30 seconds.

Wednesday
4
INDEPENDENCE DAY

1918—Thirteen new U.S. Navy destroyers—*McKean, Harding, Gridley, Maury, Williams, Crane, Hart, Ingraham, Upshur, Elliot, Thomas, Haraden*, and *Abbot*—were launched on this day.

Thursday
5

1911—Ellwood Widmer Etchells, Star-class sailing champion, boatbuilder, and designer of the Etchells 22 class keelboat, was born in Philadelphia, Pennsylvania.

Friday
6

2004—Austin Packard Farrar, yacht designer and boatbuilder, one of the pioneers in cold-molded construction, died in England.

Saturday ◑
7

1867—A crew of four oarsmen from Saint John, New Brunswick, Canada, defeated all comers at the Exhibition Regatta, Paris, France.

Sunday
8

1857—The owners of the schooner-yacht *America* gave custody of the America's Cup to the New York Yacht Club.

The rocky ledge runs far into the sea,
And on its outer point, some miles away,
The Lighthouse lifts its massive masonry,
A pillar of fire by night, of cloud by day.
—from "The Lighthouse,"
by Henry Wadsworth Longfellow

VISIBILITY OF A LIGHTHOUSE LIGHT, ACCORDING TO THE U.S. COAST GUARD

The theoretical visibility of a light in clear weather depends upon two factors, the height of the light above water, and its intensity. The height controls what is known as the geographic range, while the intensity controls what is known as the luminous range. As a rule, for the principal lights the luminous range is greater than the geographic, and the distance from which such lights are visible is limited by the earth's curvature only. Under some atmospheric conditions the glare or loom of these lights, and occasionally the light itself, may be visible far beyond the computed geographic range. On the other hand, and unfortunately more frequently, these distances may be lessened by fog, rain, snow, haze, or smoke.

NO REST FOR THE LIGHTKEEPER

The duties of the keeper should be most rigidly enforced. No keeper should be permitted to decide when is the proper time to light or extinguish his lights, but should be instructed to light his lamps at sunset, and keep the flames at their most effective height until sunrise. A failure to perform this duty strictly should be sufficient warrant for his removal.
—Report on Investigation of the Lighthouse Establishment, 1846

Untidiness will be strongly reprehended, and its continuance will subject a keeper to dismissal.
—from the 1881 Lighthouse Service Instruction

STEAM LAUNCH FROM THE U.S. REVENUE CUTTER *CORWIN*, EXPLORING THE KOWAK RIVER, ALASKA, JULY 13, 1884

All day long the river grew narrower and the current more rapid.... During the afternoon we ran into a reach of the river extending NE for about six miles; the vista was one of surpassing loveliness. Both banks were low and green in the sunshine, while beyond and partly hidden by a light mist a range of ragged mountains could be seen, lying cool and tranquil in the distance. At the end of the reach we came upon a succession of high bluffs formed by the foot-hills of the mountains running in on the river. Their sides were clothed with the sweet-smelling pine and juniper, and a narrow, rocky beach lay at their bases. Here we pitched camp.... We would have called the place Utopia, had not the mosquitoes nearly driven us wild.
—Third Lieutenant John C. Cantwell

The sea drives truth into a man like salt.
—Hilaire Belloc

JULY

Monday
9

1813—*The Life of Nelson*, by Robert Southey—the standard against which all biographies of Horatio Nelson, victor at the sea battles of the Nile, Copenhagen, and Trafalgar, are judged—was published.

Tuesday
10

1969—The trimaran *Teignmouth Electron* was found sailing herself in the Atlantic Ocean near the Azores; documents aboard suggested that her skipper, Donald Crowhurst, engaged in a nonstop singlehanded race around the world, had jumped overboard about 10 days earlier.

Wednesday
11

1991—Gerard d'Aboville got underway from Choshi, Japan, in the rowboat *Sector* on what would be the first west-to-east singlehanded crossing of the Pacific Ocean.

Thursday
12

1922 —The five-masted bark *France II*, at 418 feet the largest sailing ship ever built, was wrecked off New Caledonia.

Friday
13

1955—Eric and Susan Hiscock returned to England in the 30-foot cutter *Wanderer III* following a circumnavigation of the globe for which they would be awarded the Blue Water Medal of the Cruising Club of America.

Saturday ●
14

1926—The first navigational radiobeacon in Alaska went into commission at Cape Spencer.

Sunday
15

1880—The American Shoal Light, off Summerland Key, Florida, was illuminated for the first time.

A sea story has to be patently impossible and romanticized before it may be acceptable to great masses of the citizens.

—William McFee

TO WRITE ABOUT THE SEA AND SHIPS, ACCORDING TO HAMMOND INNES

The sea means ships of one sort or another, and to write about ships calls for technical knowledge far beyond the normal background requirements of fiction—technical knowledge of tides and weather and charts, of the theory and practice of navigation. And if it is sailing ships, then there is additionally the whole complicated assembly of spars, rigging and sails. But whether it is sail, steam, motor, or simply the manpower of oars, there is still a maze of nautical jargon that must come automatically to mind as the pen slips over the page.

FICTION SERIES ABOUT THE GOLDEN AGE OF THE ROYAL NAVY DURING THE NAPOLEONIC WARS—THE CLASSICS

The Hornblower novels, by C. S. Forester

Mr. Midshipman Hornblower; Lieutenant Hornblower; Hornblower and the Hotspur; Hornblower and the Atropos; Beat to Quarters; Ship of the Line; Flying Colours; Commodore Hornblower; Lord Hornblower; Admiral Hornblower in the West Indies

The Nathaniel Drinkwater novels, by Richard Woodman

An Eye of the Fleet; A King's Cutter; A Brig of War; The Bomb Vessel; The Corvette; 1805; Baltic Mission; In Distant Waters; A Private Revenge; Under False Colours; The Flying Squadron; Beneath the Aurora; The Shadow of the Eagle; Ebb Tide

The Aubrey/Maturin novels, by Patrick O'Brian

Master and Commander; Post Captain; HMS Surprise; The Mauritius Command; Desolation Island; The Fortune of War; The Surgeon's Mate; The Ionian Mission; Treason's Harbour; The Far Side of the World; The Reverse of the Medal; The Letter of Marque; The Thirteen-Gun Salute; The Nutmeg of Consolation; Clarissa Oakes (in the U.S.: *Truelove); The Wine-Dark Sea; The Commodore; The Yellow Admiral; The Hundred Days; Blue at the Mizzen*

The cutter *Española*, among the Western Isles, Scotland, July 18, 1921

Harbour of Mallaig. At 6 a.m. sculled over softly to the sleeping launch and deposited in the cockpit two sailing books for which the owner had expressed a desire. It was a small return for three bottles of a certain fluid manufactured in the north which we found had been put aboard us during the night as "a present from Greenock." We left at 6.30 under motor, which was going until near Eilean Castel in Eigg, where we got a fresh breeze which proved purely local, but enabled us to lie Ardnamurchan on the starboard tack. Several whales were seen blowing and sending up showers of spray as they dived. Off Ardnamurchan in a flat calm we met the north-going tide, and used motor until a new breeze, with rain, came astern, to which we set spinnaker and came into Tobermory with a flowing sheet.

—H. M. Wright

The ocean as a transcendental realm is fast disappearing from our national literature.
—John D. Seelye

JULY

Monday
16

1845—The first regatta of the New York Yacht Club was held, during which a time allowance system was used for the first time in the United States.

Tuesday
17

1840—The *Britannia*, the first transatlantic passenger steamer of the Cunard Line, arrived in Boston, Massachusetts, at the conclusion of her maiden voyage from Liverpool, England.

Wednesday
18

1932—The United States and Canada signed a treaty to develop the St. Lawrence Seaway, connecting the Great Lakes with the Atlantic Ocean.

Thursday
19

1837—The *Great Western*, the first passenger steamship specifically built for the transatlantic run, was launched in Bristol, England.

Friday
20

1979—Diana Nyad swam from the Bahamas to Florida, across 60 miles of open ocean.

Saturday
21

1899—Ernest Hemingway, author of *The Old Man and the Sea*, was born in Oak Park, Illinois.

Sunday ◐
22

1882—Artist Edward Hopper, many of whose paintings featured coastal and maritime themes, was born in Nyack, New York.

ACCORDING TO THE NATIONAL WEATHER SERVICE

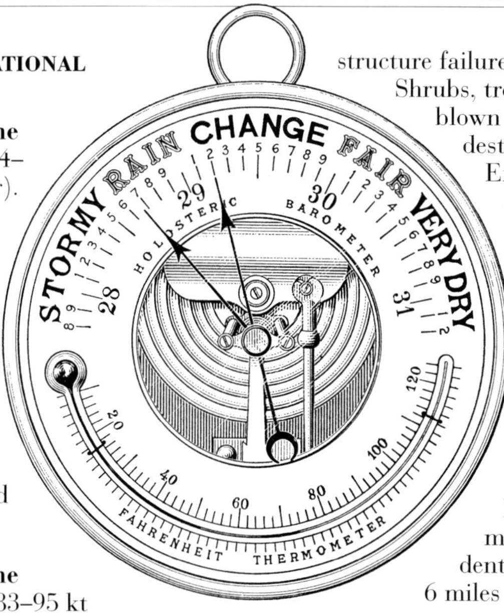

Category One Hurricane

Winds 74–95 mph (64–82 kt or 119–153 km/hr). Storm surge generally 4–5 ft above normal. No real damage to building structures. Damage primarily to unanchored mobile homes, shrubbery, and trees. Some damage to poorly constructed signs. Also, some coastal road flooding and minor pier damage.

Category Two Hurricane

Winds 96–110 mph (83–95 kt or 154–177 km/hr). Storm surge generally 6–8 ft above normal. Some roofing material, door, and window damage of buildings. Considerable damage to shrubbery and trees with some trees blown down. Considerable damage to mobile homes, poorly constructed signs, and piers. Coastal and low-lying escape routes flood 2–4 hours before arrival of the center of the hurricane. Small craft in unprotected anchorages break moorings.

Category Three Hurricane

Winds 111–130 mph (96–113 kt or 178–209 km/hr). Storm surge generally 9–12 ft above normal. Some structural damage to small residences and utility buildings with a minor amount of curtainwall failures. Damage to shrubbery and trees with foliage blown off trees and large trees blown down. Mobile homes and poorly constructed signs are destroyed. Low-lying escape routes are cut by rising water 3–5 hours before arrival of the center of the hurricane. Flooding near the coast destroys smaller structures with larger structures damaged by battering from floating debris. Terrain continuously lower than 5 ft above mean sea level may be flooded inland 8 miles (13 km) or more. Evacuation of low-lying residences within several blocks of the shoreline may be required.

Category Four Hurricane

Winds 131–155 mph (114–135 kt or 210–249 km/hr). Storm surge generally 13–18 ft above normal. More extensive curtainwall failures with some complete roof structure failures on small residences. Shrubs, trees, and all signs are blown down. Complete destruction of mobile homes. Extensive damage to doors and windows. Low-lying escape routes may be cut by rising water 3–5 hours before arrival of the center of the hurricane. Major damage to lower floors of structures near the shore. Terrain lower than 10 ft above sea level may be flooded, requiring massive evacuation of residential areas as far inland as 6 miles (10 km).

Category Five Hurricane

Winds greater than 155 mph (135 kt or 249 km/hr). Storm surge generally greater than 18 ft above normal. Complete roof failure on many residences and industrial buildings. Some complete building failures with small utility buildings blown over or away. All shrubs, trees, and signs blown down. Complete destruction of mobile homes. Severe and extensive window and door damage. Low-lying escape routes are cut by rising water 3–5 hours before arrival of the center of the hurricane. Major damage to lower floors of all structures located less than 15 ft above sea level and within 500 yards of the shoreline. Massive evacuation of residential areas on low ground within 5–10 miles (8–16 km) of the shoreline may be required.

THE 100-FOOT SCHOONER *AMORITA*, LAKE MICHIGAN, MACKINAC RACE, JULY 23, 1911

6:30 p.m.—Barometer 28.70. Terrific wind and sea.

7:00 p.m.—Took off the foresail. Barometer 28.61.

7:30 p.m.—Raining hard, blowing a gale, and heavy mist. Impossible to face wind and rain.

7:45 p.m.—Barometer 28.37 and still going down.

8:00 p.m.—Hurricane blowing.

10:20 p.m.—Arrived Mackinac Island.

—from the ship's log

O for a soft and gentle wind!
—Allan Cunningham

JULY

Monday
23

1876—The clipper ship *Young America* sailed from 50 degrees South in the Atlantic Ocean to 50 degrees South in the Pacific Ocean in the incredible time of only six days.

Tuesday
24

1883—Captain Matthew Webb, who previously had swum across the English Channel, drowned while attempting to swim through the Whirlpool Rapids, Niagara Falls.

Wednesday
25

1814—Charles Dibdin, author of "The Jolly Young Waterman," "Then Farewell My Trim-Built Wherry," "The Lass That Loves a Sailor," and other sea songs, died in Camden Town, England.

Thursday
26

2003—The largest free-floating raft-up to date, 944 boats tethered together, took place on Lake Norman, North Carolina.

Friday
27

1969—Tom McClean arrived in Blacksod Bay, Ireland, in the rowboat *Super Silver* from St. John's, Newfoundland, at the end of the first solo east-to-west crossing under oars of the Atlantic Ocean.

Saturday
28

1615—French explorer Samuel de Champlain discovered Lake Huron.

Sunday
29

1967—The aircraft carrier USS *Forrestal*, off the coast of North Vietnam, caught fire; 134 lives were lost.

ANNALS OF WOMEN IN THE U.S. COAST GUARD

19th century—Women served as lighthouse keepers.
1917—Women authorized to enlist in Coast Guard as yeomen (unofficially, yeomanettes).
1942—Coast Guard Women's Reserve, aka SPARS (Semper Paratus, Always Ready), established.
1943—Training center for enlisted SPARS established in the old Biltmore Hotel, Palm Beach, Florida; Officer Candidate School at Smith College, Northampton, Massachusetts, and later at the Coast Guard Academy, New London, Connecticut.
1943—A lieutenant (jg) in the SPARS was given command of a Loran station.
1944—The first African American woman joined the SPARS.
1947—SPARS disbanded.
1948—Last woman lighthouse keeper retired.
1949—SPARS reactivated.
early 1950s—Korean War, several former SPARS rejoined the Coast Guard.
1973—Women became eligible for the regular and reserve Coast Guard, and for enrollment in Officer Candidate School.
1976—First women enrolled at the Coast Guard Academy.
1977—First women officers and enlisted women assigned to seagoing cutters.
1977—First woman qualified as a Coast Guard aviator.
1979—First female commissioned officer given command of a Coast Guard cutter, a 95-foot patrol boat.
1980—First women graduated from the Coast Guard Academy.
1988—First enlisted woman given command of a cutter, a tugboat.

THE U.S. COAST GUARD, AN AVERAGE YEAR

Calls for assistance—more than 40,000
Merchant vessel inspections—more than 50,000
Lives saved—more than 3,000
Environmental hazard responses—more than 11,000
Aids to navigation maintained—more than 50,000
and then there were commercial fishing laws enforced, offshore drilling platforms inspected, anti–drug-smuggling patrols conducted, waterways and shipping channels kept free of ice, shipping traffic directed, antiterrorism activities, and more.

A THAMES ROWING SKIFF ON THE RIVER AVON NEAR STRATFORD, ENGLAND, AUGUST 4, 1875

We sculled about a mile, and then came to Charlcote Park, the seat of Sir Spencer Lucy. This gentleman has evidently very little sympathy for rowing men, as just at the boundary of his park, he has had a row of posts sunk right across the river. These were connected by chains, and there was also a row of floating planks just underneath the chain, kept in position by being attached to the posts. This barrier as well as another at the other end of the park, was for the purpose of preventing the deer from swimming up the river, and getting away. We could not get the boat round, as the banks were so steep, and as the chains just touched the water, we thought that if the boat was lightened sufficiently, we might perhaps be able to get over with a rush. Clarke, Fred and I therefore landed, taking the rudder off, and leaving Tom with the sculls, and George in the stern to direct him to the easiest place where the chain appeared to be an inch or two under the water. Tom made a rush at the place, and the boat glided over well, as the bow was well out of the water. —Howard Williams

To all landsmen, from youth upwards, the boat remains a piece of enchantment.
—John Ruskin

JULY/AUGUST

Monday 30

1904—In an early contest between gasoline and steam marine engines, the gasoline motorboat *Standard* (24.29 mph) defeated N. G. Herreshoff's celebrated steam launch *Swift Sure* (23.16 mph), considered to be the finest of her type.

Tuesday 31

1976—The first annual Antique and Classic Boat Rendezvous was held at Mystic Seaport Museum, Mystic, Connecticut.

Wednesday 1

1888—The first installment of the humor classic *Three Men in a Boat (Not to Mention the Dog)* was published in the monthly magazine *Home Chimes;* the collected work would be published in book form in 1889.

Thursday 2

1917—E. H. Dunning landed a Sopwith Pup on HMS *Furious*, the first landing of an aircraft on a ship actually underway.

Friday 3

1942—Mildred McAfee (Horton) became the first female commissioned officer in the U.S. Naval Reserve.

Saturday 4

Coast Guard Day

Sunday 5

1914—The British cable ship *Telconia* cut through all five of Germany's undersea telegraph cables, thus destroying that country's overseas communications.

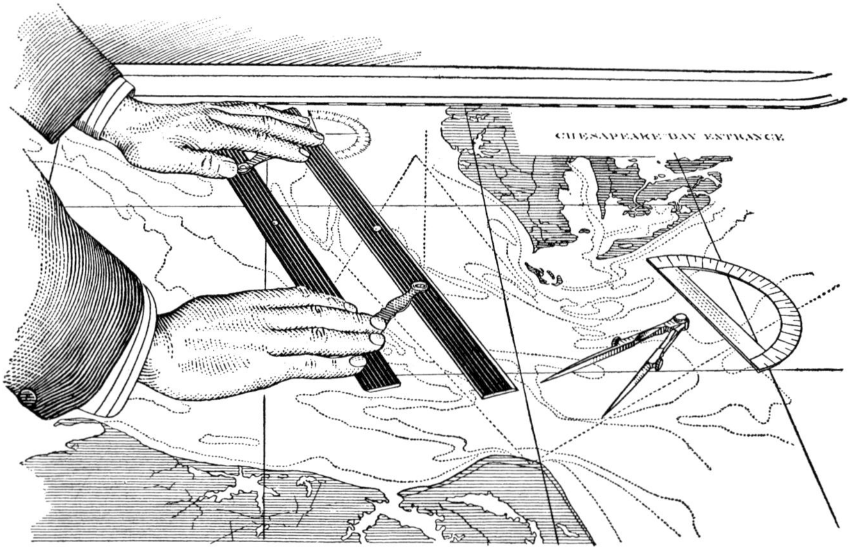

IF YOU RUN AGROUND

Know state of tide.
Sound all around.
Form a plan—be careful.
Have everyone on board act together.
Lay out anchors if it can be done—at once.
If bow on, try to keep stern free.
When tide and wind are right, trim tanks, drop weights. Work the vessel free.

EFFECT OF WIND AND BAROMETER ON SOUNDINGS

Keep in mind that at low tide a strong wind blowing seaward from a bay or cove and an unusually high barometer may cause the water to fall below the chart's indicated depth.

CHART SCALES

Chart scales indicate the ratio of a given distance on the chart to the actual distance it represents on the earth. A scale of 1:80,000 or 1/80,000 means that 1 unit (usually 1 inch) on the chart represents 80,000 units on the earth.

A small-scale chart is one covering a relatively large area. A large-scale chart is one covering a relatively small area.

To determine nautical miles per inch, divide the reciprocal of the scale by 72,913.39.

To determine statute miles per inch, divide the reciprocal of the scale by 63,360.

To determine inches per nautical mile, multiply the scale by 79,913.39.

To determine inches per statute mile, multiply the scale by 63,360.

CHART SCALES, A MEMORY AID

Small scale, small detail
Large scale, large detail.

THE 10-FOOT DOUBLE-PADDLE CANOE *NESSMUK NO. 1*, AKA *WOOD DRAKE*, FULTON CHAIN OF LAKES, ADIRONDACK MOUNTAINS, NEW YORK

Then it struck me that I had a seven mile start toward Blue Mountain Lake, with such weather as I might not get again for a month. True, I had no supplies, but they could be had at Arnold's, some two miles above, and I struck across and up the lake for Arnold's place. Got some lunch, arranged my duffle for a trip, and paddled out for a log camp I knew of at the foot of Fifth Lake. It was getting dusk when I struck the Inlet, and by the time I reached the camp it was nearly dark; but I found the camp in good condition. There was fresh browse and plenty of dry birch wood, with a roof invulnerable to rain. I had no tea or coffee, or any sort of dish; but I foraged an old tomato can and made a pot of hemlock tea, had a glorious fire, and a night just such as a woodsman loves. There was not a soul within miles of me, and the shriek of the steam whistle was afar off, beyond the keenest earshot. The owls were plentier than usual, and in exceptionally good voice, while a loon, just above in the Fifth, kept up his strange wild cries at intervals through the night.

—"Nessmuk" (George Washington Sears)

The only mission of a seaman's calling is to keep ships' keels off the ground.
—Joseph Conrad

AUGUST

Monday
6

1878—The Revenue Cutter *Chase*, the last sailing cutter built for the Revenue Service, forerunner of the U.S. Coast Guard, was launched.

Tuesday
7

1992—The luxury liner *Queen Elizabeth 2*, aka *QE2*, ran aground off Massachusetts.

Wednesday
8

1813—The schooners *Hamilton* and *Scourge* of the U.S. Navy capsized and sank in a squall on Lake Ontario with the loss of more than 80 lives. The two vessels, still virtually intact, were located by side-scan sonar in 1973.

Thursday
9

1942—Three heavy cruisers—USS *Astoria*, USS *Quincy*, and USS *Vincennes*—were sunk by Japanese warships off Savo, Solomon Islands.

Friday
10

1918—The German submarine *U-117* sank nine fishing vessels—*Aleda May*, *William H. Starbuck*, *Progress*, *Reliance*, *Earl & Nellie*, *Cruiser*, *Old Time*, *Mary E. Sennett*, and *Katie L. Palmer*—in the western Atlantic Ocean.

Saturday
11

1921—Alex Haley, career coast-guardsman, author of the novel *Roots*, was born in Ithaca, New York.

Sunday ●
12

1996—*The Wall Street Journal* reported that hundreds of thousands of flip-flops (sandals) had washed ashore on the Cocos and Keeling Islands, Indian Ocean.

LEARN TO SAIL BEFORE YOU MOTOR, SAYS E. F. KNIGHT

If a novice wishes to make himself a sailor he should dispense with the auxiliary motor until he has mastered certain problems—for example, the way to come up to his moorings under canvas. Some young men make a practice, when entering their port, of lowering their sails, to approach their moorings under motor power. For such a one, who has not learnt his job properly, the day is sure to come when his motor will suddenly break down, as motors will; he will then have his canvas only to rely upon, and he is likely to make a pretty mess of things in his attempts to pick up his mooring buoy, possibly in a crowded anchorage with a strong tide running.

I prefer a sail-boat to a motor-boat, and it is my belief that boat-sailing is a finer, more difficult, and sturdier art than running a motor.

—Jack London

THE THREE FUNDAMENTAL POSITIONS OF SAILING

Into the wind (aka on the wind, close-hauled, beating, strapped down, into the wind)—generally, the safest

Across the wind (aka off the wind, reaching, running free)—generally, the fastest

With the wind (aka before the wind, downwind)—generally, the most dangerous

He is the best sailor who can steer within the fewest points of the wind.

—Henry David Thoreau

THE CUTTER *BLUE BIRD*, NORFOLK BROADS, ENGLAND, AUGUST 16, 1911

Thanks to the pointing qualities of *Blue Bird*, I managed to sail down the New Cut, a perfectly straight and narrow canal of over 3 miles in length, impossible to tack in, connecting the Waverney with the Yare. The slant of wind barely allowed me to sail through, though I luffed at every puff. Some other boats which followed had to tow. I left Somerleyton at 10.30, but had to moor and wait till 3.15 to pass through Herringfleet swing bridge. A short way on, across the cut, is another bridge (with a shilling toll) that lifts like the Tower Bridge. Reedham, a village at the end of the New Cut, is not a very good place for mooring, the banks being shallow, but I found a resting-place for the night further down, where some other boats lay among the reeds in the Yare. Distance run, about 4½ miles.

—Walter E. Ledger

I do not know anything more glorious or exciting than to stand at the tiller of a noble yacht, with a slashing breeze making her leap through the seas.
—Vanderdecken

AUGUST

Monday
13

1779—In the worst American naval defeat until Pearl Harbor in 1941, a Continental squadron of more than 40 vessels was defeated by a British squadron in Penobscot Bay near Castine, Maine.

Tuesday
14

1941—President Franklin Roosevelt and Prime Minister Winston Churchill, meeting in Placentia Bay, Newfoundland, aboard USS *Augusta* and HMS *Prince of Wales*, signed the Atlantic Charter.

Wednesday
15

1925—The first Fastnet Race got underway from the Isle of Wight, England, to the Fastnet Rock off Ireland, and back; *Jolie Brise*, a converted Le Havre pilot boat, took first place.

Thursday
16

1879—A powerful hurricane struck the northeast coast of the United States, wrecking more than 100 large and 200 small vessels between North Carolina and Maine.

Friday
17

1915—A hurricane with winds gusts to 120 mph and a 12-foot storm surge struck Galveston, Texas; more than 275 lives were lost.

Saturday
18

1938—The Thousand Islands Bridge over the St. Lawrence River, connecting New York State with the Canadian province of Ontario, was dedicated.

Sunday
19

1939—*Bluebird K4*, driven by Malcolm Campbell, set a world propeller-driven water-speed record of 141.74 mph, on Coniston Water, Cumbria, England.

A WEEK AT SEA, ACCORDING TO JEROME K. JEROME

A sea trip does you good when you are going to have a couple of months of it, but, for a week, it is wicked. You start on Monday with the idea implanted in your bosom that you are going to enjoy yourself. You wave an airy adieu to the boys on shore, light your biggest pipe, and swagger about the deck as if you were Captain Cook, Sir Francis Drake, and Christopher Columbus all rolled into one. On Tuesday, you wish you hadn't come. On Wednesday, Thursday, and Friday, you wish you were dead. On Saturday, you are able to swallow a little beef tea, and to sit up on deck, and answer with a wan, sweet smile when kind-hearted people ask you how you feel now. On Sunday, you begin to walk about again, and take solid food. And on Monday morning, as, with your bag and umbrella in your hand, you stand by the gunwale, waiting to step ashore, you begin to thoroughly like it.

GINGER IN ITS VARIOUS FORMS IS AN EXCELLENT NATURAL SEASICKNESS PREVENTIVE

Ginger ale and its stronger cousin, ginger beer (nonalcoholic)
Candied ginger
Ginger snaps
Ground ginger tea
Ginger tablets (available from health-food stores)

IF YOU BECOME SEASICK

Vomit to leeward; wear a safety harness if the rail is low.

Lie down in a non-claustrophobia–inducing, well-ventilated place, preferably on deck in the fresh air.

Keep warm.

Drink small amounts of liquid as frequently as possible to keep from becoming dehydrated.

THE CONSEQUENCE OF SEASICKNESS, SLANG OF THE SAILOR

Ralphing
Searching for Ensign Ralph
Praying to the porcelain god
Chumming for the whales
Yawning in Technicolor
Liquid laughing
Blowing chunks
Mustering your bag

THE PACKET SHIP *PACIFIC*, MID-ATLANTIC OCEAN, WESTBOUND FOR NEW YORK, AUGUST 20, 1832

Calm, utter calm—a roasting August sun, a waveless sea, the sails flapping idly against our mast. Wrote my journal, walked about and in the evening danced merrily, quadrilles and country dances. Fairly danced myself tired and came to bed. But oh! not to sleep—mercy what a night! The wind blowing like mad, the ship pitching, bouncing, shuddering, creaking and groaning, till ten o'clock, when I got up and was going to see how near drowning we were, when Dall, who was lying awake too, implored me to lie down again. Lay till daylight, the gale was increasing furiously, boxes, chairs, beds and their contents rolling about in glorious confusion.

—Fanny Kemble

How holy people look when they are sea-sick!
—Samuel Butler

AUGUST

Monday ◐
20

1977—A replica of the *Turtle*, David Bushnell's experimental submarine developed during the American Revolutionary War, was christened in Essex, Connecticut.

Tuesday
21

1918—Ensign Charles Hazeltine Hammann, U.S. Navy, flying a seaplane, rescued a downed pilot in the Adriatic Sea, for which he became the first naval aviator to be awarded the Congressional Medal of Honor.

Wednesday
22

1994—The U.S. Coast Guard icebreaker *Polar Sea* became the first U.S. surface vessel to reach the North Pole.

Thursday
23

1890—Alfred ("Alf") Fullerton Loomis, yachtsman, author of the column "Under the Lee of the Longboat" in *Yachting* magazine and of *Ocean Racing* and *Ranging the Maine Coast*, among other books, was born in Connecticut.

Friday
24

1905—The four-masted bark *Susquehannah*, one of the finest of the downeaster type, was abandoned at sea after her seams opened up during a storm.

Saturday
25

1888—The *Great Eastern*, the largest passenger steamer of her time, was beached before being broken up near Liverpool, England.

Sunday
26

1791—John Fitch was granted a patent for a working steamboat.

THE 21-FOOT YAWL *KATE*, NORTH SEA OFF YARMOUTH, ENGLAND, SEPTEMBER 1, 1869

[The sea] had a very ugly appearance, taking the form of immense curling breakers, from eighteen to twenty feet high. The excitement of running over these was glorious; the boat ran right on the very edge of some, conveying the idea that, if a plumb-line could be dropped from the bowsprit, it would touch nothing for twenty feet, the decks being a mass of white water as the wave broke, and *The Kate* subsided gracefully into the hollow. The only comparison that I can make to running before a heavy sea is that of riding across country on a horse that jumps high and wide; the feeling is the same in each case, but only momentary in the jump, whereas the boat may run just on the verge of the wave for several minutes together. The impression is that of never coming down, or a sort of flying in the air, which I well remember, on one occasion, when riding my Arab horse "Monarch" on a sky-larking jumping expedition with a number of officers of her Majesty's 51st and other corps. The horse was jumping very wide, and at last culminated his efforts in a splendid leap, which measured over thirty feet.

—E. E. Middleton

ACCORDING TO THE *GUINNESS WORLD RECORDS*

Busiest port—Rotterdam, Netherlands

Deepest manned ocean descent—35,797 feet, bathyscaph *Trieste*, Challenger Deep, Mariana Trench

Fastest propeller-driven boat—*Miss Budweiser*, hydroplane, 220.493 mph, 2004

Fastest submarines—Russian Alpha class, nuclear-powered, 40 knots

Greatest distance by pedal boat—4,660 miles, Hawaii to Japan, by Kenichi Horie, 1993

Largest aircraft carriers—Nimitz class, U.S. Navy, 1,092 feet long

Largest car ferry—*Ulysses*, Irish Ferries, 686 feet long, can carry 1,342 cars, built 2000

Largest cargo vessel—*Jahre Viking*, tanker, 1,504 feet long, 555,843 tons

Largest battleships ever—*Yamato* and *Musashi*, Japan, World War II, 863 feet long, 71,111 tons

Largest passenger liner—*Queen Mary 2*, 1,132 feet long, 150,000 tons, three times larger than *Titanic*, built 2003

Largest propeller—29.5 feet diameter, 93.5 tons, six blades, cast in the United Kingdom, 1997

Largest sail—genoa by Doyle Sailmakers for yacht *Mirabella*, 19,730 square feet

Largest sailing ship—*France II*, 418 feet long, 5,806 tons, built 1911

Largest paddlewheel steamboat—*American Queen*, 418 feet long, built 1995

Largest yacht—Saudi Arabian royal yacht *Abdul Aziz*, 482 feet long, built 1984

Tallest mast—295-foot mainmast, yacht *Mirabella*, built 2003

Fastest circumnavigation of the globe in a power vessel—*Cable and Wireless Adventurer*, 115 feet long; 74 days, 20 hours, 58 minutes, 30 seconds, 1998

Nothing more clearly indicates the taste of a mercantile community than its ships.
—*Boston Daily Atlas,* December 21, 1850

AUG/SEPT

Monday
27
SUMMER BANK HOLIDAY / UK

1859—Wildcat drillers working for E. L. Drake struck oil near Titusville, Pennsylvania, thus beginning the development of the commercial oil industry in the United States and beginning the end of the whale-oil fishery.

Tuesday ○
28

1872—The National Association of Amateur Oarsmen, now the United States Rowing Association, the first national organization for amateur team sports, was established.

Wednesday
29

1924—The raceboat *Rainbow IV* won the 1924 Gold Cup in Detroit, Michigan.

Thursday
30

1956—*MLB 36544*, the last of the U.S. Coast Guard's legendary 36-foot self-righting motor lifeboats, was launched at the Coast Guard Yard, Curtis Bay, Maryland.

Friday
31

1890—In the first recorded seagoing drug bust, the U.S. Revenue Cutter *Wolcott* seized a shipment of opium aboard the steamer *George E. Starr* in the Strait of Juan de Fuca.

Saturday
1

2000—The *Ulysses*, a mammoth 686-foot ferry with a capacity of 1,342 cars, was launched by Irish Ferries.

Sunday
2

1945—Representatives of Japan signed surrender documents on board the battleship USS *Missouri*, moored in Tokyo Bay, thus ending World War II.

ALFRED BASIL LUBBOCK (1876–1944)

Many of the authors who chronicled the golden era of sailing ships were educated men of privilege who sailed, if only briefly, before the mast in the declining days of sail. Basil Lubbock, whose father was the son of an English baronet, was one of them. Born in 1876, educated at Eton, he sailed to Canada and, after climbing the Chilcoot Trail, participated in the great Klondike gold rush. He then sailed as an ordinary seaman around Cape Horn from San Francisco back to England aboard a four-masted bark and wrote a book about the experience; later, he served aboard a full-rigged ship. Lubbock fought in South Africa during the Boer War and in India and France during World War I, after which he returned home and became absorbed in historical research and recording the memories of old-timers who had gone to sea in sail. Over the years, writing in a bare-bones, matter-of-fact style notable for its technical accuracy, he published a series of books on sailing ships and shipping, many of which are still in print.

HARMSWORTH TROPHY SPEEDBOAT RACES, LAKE ST. CLAIR, MICHIGAN, SEPTEMBER 3, 1932

When I stepped out into that dark morning at five o'clock, I felt sure there would be no race, no spectators, nothing. A pitiless cold rain was driving down and I knew that the course would be a sea of whitecaps. I felt like I was a lone figure of the night, standing thin and gaunt and cold against the black sky. I stepped into my car and drove down to the lake. I can't quite tell the feeling that swept through me at what I saw—probably a thousand stabbing, bobbing, disappearing lights out across the lake moving in an almost endless string toward a common goal, the Harmsworth course. I knew what that meant. And I was amazed. They were the boats—canoes, rowboats, dingeys [sic], cockleshells, sailboats, cruisers, yachts, runabouts—loaded to the gunwales with part of the race-mad crowds that throng to see these races every year. From a black wind-broken sky the rains came. And through that dim night the drenched pageant moved across an angry sea like a specter.

—J. Lee Barrett

The high degree of specialization in the craftsmanship of the sea, and of differentiation between it and anything to be found on land, alike make the writing of true nautical literature a task for seamen alone.

—Lincoln Colcord

A FEW OF THE SCORES OF BOOKS BY BASIL LUBBOCK

Round the Horn Before the Mast, 1902
The China Clippers, 1914
The Colonial Clippers, 1921
The Blackwall Frigates, 1922
The Log of the Cutty Sark, 1924
The Western Ocean Packets, 1925
The Last of the Windjammers, in two volumes, 1927–29
The Down Easters, 1929
The Nitrate Clippers, 1932
The Opium Clippers, 1933
Coolie Ships and Oil Sailers, 1935
The Arctic Whalers, 1937

And further, by these, my son, be admonished: of making many books there is no end....
—Ecclesiastes 12:12

SEPTEMBER

Monday
3
LABOR DAY/ US & CANADA

1944—Alfred Basil Lubbock, author of *The China Clippers, The Down Easters, The Log of the Cutty Sark*, and other books about sailing ships and the sea, died at Monk's Orchard, Blatchington, Seaford, Sussex, England.

Tuesday ◑
4

1922—The raceboat *Packard Chriscraft* won the 1922 Gold Cup in Detroit, Michigan.

Wednesday
5

1914—The German submarine U-21 sank HMS *Pathfinder*, the first warship lost to a submarine.

Thursday
6

1907—The luxury liner *Lusitania* got underway from London, England, for New York on her maiden voyage.

Friday
7

1789—James Fenimore Cooper, author of *The History of the Navy of the United States, The Pilot: A Tale of the Sea*, and *Ned Myers, or, A Life Before the Mast*, was born in Burlington, New Jersey.

Saturday
8

1973—The first fully crewed round-the-world race, the Whitbread, with 17 yachts from 7 nations, got underway from Portsmouth, England.

Sunday
9

1833—The first naval drydock built by the U.S. government was completed in Boston, Massachusetts.

THE KETCH *TYPHOON*, OFF THE COAST OF SPAIN, BAY OF BISCAY, SEPTEMBER 12, 1920

Foggy. Barograph going up like a stepladder.

2:30A.M. Breeze springs up from S. and after a while settles to W. x S. Course due S.

8:50. Strange ketch rigged craft looms up through fog, dead ahead, bound E.—a husky double-ender like some of the Scandinavian craft, with white top strake and brown sides. Carrying everything she has—dirty white sails wing and wing, topsails and brown square sail. Soon lost in fog.

9:10. Fox on watch yells "Land on starboard bow!" As we approach cautiously this proves to be a rocky promontory with the swell breaking into fantastic lace work along the base, which is abrupt and apparently without outlying rocks. As we approach, a plateau takes form with the silhouette of a solitary horse grazing on the skyline and on beyond to port, a cove with romantic yellow sandy beach, just visible through the fog. Off farther to port a small rocky island and later high mountains beyond. Stood in to about 300 yd. from point and came about on port tack, to beat along within sight of the coast till we identify something to give us our position. No large scale charts. Not an advisable way to explore a foreign coast but lots of fun.

—William Washburn Nutting

One night came on a hurricane,
The sea was mountains rolling
When Barney Buntline turned his quid,
And said to Billy Bowling:
"A strong nor-wester's blowing, Bill;
Hark! don't ye hear it roar, now?
Lord help 'em, how I pities them
Unhappy folks on shore now!"

—from "The Sailor's Consolation," by Charles Dibdin

I once knew a writer who, after saying beautiful things about the sea, passed through a Pacific hurricane, and he became a changed man.

—Joshua Slocum

IF YOU ARE CAUGHT OUT IN A STORM

In the Northern Hemisphere the wind rotates around the storm center in an anticlockwise direction.

If the wind hauls to the right, the vessel is in the right or dangerous zone—run close hauled on the starboard tack; if obliged to lie to, do so on the starboard tack.

If the wind hauls to the left, the vessel is in the left or navigable zone—run with the wind on the starboard quarter; if obliged to lie to, do so on the port tack.

If the wind remains steady, the vessel is in the path of the storm center—get the wind on the starboard quarter and keep that compass course; if obliged to lie to, do so on a tack that the wind and sea will draw aft.

—from *Small Boat Navigation*, by F. W. Sterling, 1917

How inappropriate to call this planet Earth when it is clearly Ocean.
—Arthur C. Clarke

SEPTEMBER

Monday
10

1754—William Bligh, commander of HMS *Bounty* when she was taken by mutineers, was born in Plymouth, Devon, England.

Tuesday ●
11

1960—Hurricane Donna struck Charleston, South Carolina, with wind gusts of over 120 mph.

Wednesday
12

1792—A court martial was convened aboard HMS *Duke* in Portsmouth Harbor, England, to determine the fate of nine captured mutineers from HMS *Bounty*.

Thursday
13 FIRST DAY OF ROSH HASHANAH

1988—Hurricane Gilbert struck the Cayman Islands; the barometric pressure at its center fell to 26.13 inches, a record to date for a hurricane in the Caribbean, Gulf of Mexico, and Atlantic Ocean.

Friday
14

1939—The British destroyers *Faulknor*, *Firedrake*, and *Foxhound*, operating in the North Atlantic west of the Hebrides, sank a German submarine (*U-39*), the first ships to do so in World War II.

Saturday
15

1859—The clipper ship *Mastiff*, on a voyage from San Francisco to Hong Kong, caught fire, burned, and sank.

Sunday
16

1928—Hurricane San Felipe, one of the largest to date, caused Lake Okeechobee, Florida, to overflow; approximately 2,000 people lost their lives.

IF YOU WANT TO LEARN HOW TO TALK LIKE A PIRATE...

You can't do any better than study a typical rant from Long John Silver: "Flint was cap'n; I was quartermaster, along of my timber leg. The same broadside I lost my leg, old Pew lost his deadlights. It was a master surgeon, him that ampytated me—out of college and all—Latin by the bucket, and what not; but he was hanged like a dog, and sun-dried like the rest, at Corso Castle. That was Roberts' men, that was, and comed of changing names to their ships—ROYAL FORTUNE and so on. Now, what a ship was christened, so let her stay, I says. So it was with the CASSANDRA, as brought us all safe home from Malabar, after England took the viceroy of the Indies; so it was with the old WALRUS, Flint's old ship, as I've seen amuck with the red blood and fit to sink with gold.... Where's all England's men now? I dunno. Where's Flint's? Why, most on 'em aboard here, and glad to get the duff—been begging before that, some on 'em. Old Pew, as had lost his sight, and might have thought shame, spends twelve hundred pound in a year, like a lord in Parliament. Where is he now? Well, he's dead now and under hatches."

—from *Treasure Island*,
by Robert Louis Stevenson

When angry, count four; when very angry, swear.

—Mark Twain

Profanity is the commonest sin of the boatmen, and they blaspheme in cold blood.

—Ben Perley Poore

THE CUTTER *VALA*, SOUTHWEST OF BREST, FRANCE, SEPTEMBER 16, 1933

01.00. Anxious to fix our position accurately before making coast with jury rudder, as D.R. obviously very uncertain. Got time signal from wireless at noon for the first time.

13.30. As I was taking meridian sight, S.S. *Staffordshire*, Liverpool, passed us very close. Hailed her for our position which she very promptly semaphored, but though she was going dead slow we were practically becalmed and unfortunately could not read it in time. To our surprise, however, this very courteous vessel stopped, turned round and came back to give us through a megaphone 47°41' N. 6°20' W. Creach Light bearing N. 48 E. 68 miles, an act of extreme kindness which we very much appreciated.

—D. Kemsley

WORD POWER

There is one language for the pulpit, and another for on board ship, and, in either situation, a man must make use of those terms most likely to produce the necessary effect upon his listeners.... It is not here as in the scriptures, "Do this, and he doeth it"; but it is "Do this, d—n your eyes," and then it is done directly. The order to do just carries the weight of a cannon-shot, but it wants the propelling power—the d—n is the gunpowder which sets it flying in the execution of its duty.

—from *Peter Simple*,
by Captain Frederick Marryat

I never yet heard a real conversation among seamen that would bear full reproduction in print.
—James Runciman

SEPTEMBER

Monday
17

1949—The Great Lakes cruise ship *Noronic* caught fire and burned at the dock in Toronto, Canada; 118 lives were lost.

Tuesday
18

1886—A proposal for a one-design sailing class, the first ever, was published in the *Irish Times*, leading, the following year, to the establishment of the Water Wag class.

Wednesday ◐
19

Talk Like a Pirate Day

Thursday
20

1870—Walter Brown of Massachusetts was granted a patent for a sliding seat to be fitted in a rowboat to increase the efficiency of the rower.

Friday
21

1957—The German auxiliary training bark *Pamir*, one of the last of the Cape Horners, sank with the loss of 80 lives during a storm in the Atlantic Ocean.

Saturday
22 YOM KIPPUR

1925—The Marblehead Model Yacht Club, one of the most active, was founded in Marblehead, Massachusetts.

Sunday
23 AUTUMNAL EQUINOX

1875—Women's rowing, the oldest surviving program of its type, was established at Wellesley College, Wellesley, Massachusetts.

A SHOP FOR BUILDING A BOAT

Warmth in winter, coolth in summer

Adequate light and ventilation

Source of electricity

Large enough door for getting materials in and the boat out when it is completed

Room to walk around the hull and to work on it, to store materials, and to maneuver materials into place, especially when bending wood

Eyeball room—that is, enough space to stand off at a distance to check what you have done for accuracy

Space for a workbench, and to set up tools if you will be using stationary machinery

A table for rolling out the plans

BOATBUILDING PLANS CONSIST OF THESE

Lines plan—a scale drawing showing the shape of the hull: the profile, a view from the side; the half-breadth, a view from above; and the body, a view of the cross sections

Offsets—a table of dimensions used to redraw, or "loft," the lines full size

Sail plan—a drawing showing shapes and dimensions of the spars, the rigging, and the sails

Construction plan—views of the interior of the hull showing the various parts (keel, keelson, frames, transom, centerboard, deck beams, planking, etc.) that are required to build the boat

Specifications—a list of various pieces and parts indicating sizes, breaking strengths, part numbers, designer preferences, etc.

MINIMUM SPACE IN WHICH TO BUILD A BOAT WITH REASONABLE ACCESSIBILITY, ACCORDING TO HOWARD CHAPELLE

1½ times the length of the hull

4 times the beam

1½ times the height from the bottom of the keel to the top of the cabinhouse.

THE 28-FOOT CUTTER *TERN*, ENGLISH CHANNEL, SEPTEMBER 24, 1896

She dished up several small seas with her long low counter, but soon after midnight sea was so heavy and irregular that she was almost out of hand. While I was waiting for a chance to heave her to, a great sea came over the taffrail, completely burying the vessel. I was nearly taken overboard, and the cockpit was filled to the coamings. She broached-to, and I expected that the next sea would finish her. But luckily it only partly broke on board, and then there was a smooth during which I got in the slack of the mainsheet and all fast before she began to pay off again. Headsails were already aback, so I lashed helm a-lee, and she lay fairly quiet. Pumped ship. Had brandy, bread, and a chop, and felt better for it. About 3.30 a.m. crawled along deck and furled staysail. The steering and pumping had kept me warm, but now, sitting in the well—of course, soaked to the skin—the cold wind seemed to blow clean through me.

—Claud Worth

If there is anything more interesting to watch than the construction of a small boat I should like to hear about it.
—William Atkin

SEPTEMBER

Monday
24

1876—Hallett's Point Reef, a navigational obstruction in Hell's Gate, New York, was demolished with dynamite.

Tuesday
25

1837—The racing gig *Wave* took first place for the third year in the New York Amateur Boat Club Association regatta at Castle Garden.

Wednesday ○
26

1931—The keel was laid in Newport News, Virginia, for the USS *Ranger*, the first ship designed and constructed from the keel up as an aircraft carrier.

Thursday
27

1942—In a battle in the South Atlantic between the Liberty ship *Stephen Hopkins* and the German raider *Stier*, both ships sank.

Friday
28

1891—Herman Melville, author of *Moby-Dick, Redburn, White Jacket*, and *Billy Budd*, died in New York City.

Saturday
29

1994—The ferry *Estonia* capsized and sank in the Baltic Sea between Sweden and Finland; more than 850 lives were lost.

Sunday
30

1799—The frigate *Essex*, the first U.S. naval ship to enter the Pacific Ocean, was launched in Salem, Massachusetts.

THE 40-FOOT CRUISING LAUNCH *NARCISSUS*, OFF THE MASSACHUSETTS NORTH SHORE, OCTOBER 3, 1903

Along by Cape Ann we fell in with a number of fishing schooners, and as we passed Thatchers Island we could see way out to sea a large number of vessels apparently fishing by the light of bonfires.... After passing outside the Dry Salvages, I turned in, as the Commodore, by which title Mr. [Walter] Burgess is commonly known, kindly offered to navigate for a few hours. Shortly before midnight I was awakened by the Commodore, who informed me that we were disabled, and, going to the stern, could see trailing along behind us in the moonlight what appeared to be a sea-serpent, but which to my great disappointment proved to be only the cork floats of a common fish-net which we had picked up on our propeller. We were so far from shore that we had no idea of finding such things. This looked discouraging, but having long ago foreseen the possibility of such an accident I was prepared for it, and after a delay of only about a half-hour we went on our way rejoicing. —Charles A. French

THE COLOR OF GLUE

White PVA (Elmer's, etc.)—dries clear
Light yellow PVA (Titebond, Elmer's Carpenter's)—dries darker yellow
Urea-formaldehyde (Weldwood)—dries brown
Resorcinol—dries reddish-purple
Polyurethane—some types dry amber; some dry clear
Epoxy—most types dry clear; some dry amber

WATER RESISTANCE OF GLUES

White PVA—neither water resistant nor waterproof
Yellow PVA—neither water resistant nor waterproof
Yellow PVA, Type II—short-exposure water resistant
Yellow PVA, Type III—long-exposure water resistant
Urea-formaldehyde—long-exposure water resistant
Polyurethane—long-exposure water resistant
Resorcinol—waterproof
Epoxy—waterproof

They went to sea in a sieve, they did;
In a sieve they went to sea:
In spite of all their friends could say,
On a winter's morn, on a stormy day,
In a sieve they went to sea.

—Edward Lear

The notion that modern boat construction materials are immortal is baldly stupid. Everything breaks and is eventually thrown away—and even morons these days come to understand that there is no "away."

—George Putz

GLUE—A FEW GENERAL POINTS

Most glues will produce a joint that is as strong or stronger than the wood they join; however, hot-melt glue, contact cement, and paste with a vegetable base won't.

Use glue only in bare-wood joints. Gluing together painted or otherwise coated surfaces creates a bond only with the coatings; when they break free from the underlying surfaces, your glued joint will be finished.

On a boat, use only waterproof glue in joints that will come in contact with water, however briefly; use at least water-resistant glue everywhere else.

Water can float a boat or sink it.
—old proverb

OCTOBER

Monday
1

1880—John Philip Sousa was appointed director of the U.S. Marine Corps Band.

Tuesday
2

1942—The liner *Queen Mary*, serving as a troop transport, ran down the British cruiser *Curaçao*, cutting her in two; 338 lives were lost.

Wednesday ◑
3

1970—The National Oceanic and Atmospheric Administration (NOAA) was established.

Thursday
4

1985—The USCGC *Taney*, off the coast of Virginia, seized a barge loaded with 16 tons of marijuana.

Friday
5

1864—A cyclone struck Calcutta, India; of approximately 200 major seagoing vessels driven ashore, most were unsalvageable.

Saturday
6

1917—An Act of Congress made it unlawful to sell alcoholic beverages to men in uniform.

Sunday
7

1816—The *Washington*, the first double-decked steamboat on the western rivers, arrived in New Orleans, Louisiana.

FROM THE RULES FOR THE REGULATION OF THE NAVY OF THE UNITED COLONIES OF NORTH-AMERICA, 1775

The Commanders of all ships and vessels belonging to the Thirteen United Colonies are strictly required to shew in themselves a good example of honor and virtue to their officers and men.

He [a good captain] should make the day his night and be awake the greater part of the night, always sleep in his clothes, so as to be promptly on hand for accidents that may happen.

—Samuel de Champlain

If you are to command, show yourself a leader, not by talk, but by action.

—Thomas Fleming Day

USS *SARATOGA*, AT ANCHOR, MONROVIA, LIBERIA, OCTOBER 13, 1843

A rainy morning. Last night we were all roused from sleep by the sea coming into the starboard air-ports. We of the larboard side laughed at the misfortune of our comrades, and closed our own ports, without taking the precaution to screw them in. Half an hour afterwards, a very heavy swell assailed us on the larboard, beat in all the loose ports, and deluged the rooms. I found myself suddenly awakened and cooled by a cataract of water pouring over me. Out jumped the larboard sleepers, in dripping night-gear, and shouted lustily for lights, buckets, and swabs; while the starboard gentlemen laughed long and loud, in their turn. —Horatio Bridge

NAVAL OFFICERS MUST BEHAVE THUS, SAID JOHN PAUL JONES, 1775

It is by no means enough that an officer of the navy should be a capable mariner. He must be that, of course, but also a great deal more. He should be as well a gentleman of liberal education, refined manners, punctilious courtesy, and the nicest sense of personal honor. He should be the soul of tact, patience, justice, firmness, and charity. No meritorious act of a subordinate should escape his attention or be left to pass without its reward, even if the reward is only a word of approval. Conversely, he should not be blind to a single fault in any subordinate, though, at the same time, he should be quick and unfailing to distinguish error from malice, thoughtlessness from incompetency, and well meant shortcoming from heedless or stupid blunder.

The stately ship, with all her daring band,
To skilful Albert owned the chief command;
Though trained in boisterous elements, his mind
Was yet by soft humanity refined;
Each joy of wedded love at home he knew,
Abroad, confest the father of his crew!
Brave, liberal, just! the calm domestic scene
Had o'er his temper breathed a gay serene:
Him science taught by mystic lore to trace
The planets wheeling in eternal race;
To mark the ship in floating balance held,
By earth attracted, and by seas repelled;
Or point her devious track through climes unknown
That leads to every shore and every zone.

—from "The Shipwreck," by William Falconer

No one is lonelier than a sailing ship captain.
—Alan Villiers

OCTOBER

Monday
8
THANKSGIVING / CANADA
COLUMBUS DAY / US

1949—A bottle with a note in it from the U.S. Hydrographic Office was found in Japan's Inland Sea, 14 months after it had been thrown overboard from a ship off Hawaii, 5,900 nautical miles away.

Tuesday
9

2003—The 140-foot ketch *Mari Cha IV* set a transatlantic crossing record to date for a monohull under sail of 6 days, 17 hours, 52 minutes, 39 seconds, from Ambrose Light, New York, to the Lizard, England.

Wednesday
10

1900—The *Eleanor A. Percy*, the second six-masted schooner (the *George W. Wells* was the first), was launched in Bath, Maine.

Thursday ●
11

1945—A typhoon struck the coast of Okinawa; 222 U.S. Navy small ships and landing craft were beached, 12 were sunk.

Friday
12

1823—Charles Macintosh of Glasgow, Scotland, began selling waterproof rain gear—known to this day as macs—made from rubberized cloth, a process for the manufacture of which he invented.

Saturday
13

1775—The Continental Congress enacted the first legislation involving an American navy.

Sunday
14

1812—Work began on the Regent's Canal, which would link the Grand Union Canal with the River Thames, London, England.

THE QUADRUPLE-SCREW TURBINE STEAMER *LEVIATHAN*, CHERBOURG, FRANCE, TO NEW YORK, SOUVENIR LOG, VOYAGE NO. 17, WEST, OCTOBER 1924

Departure from Cherbourg 9:22 p.m., Oct. 16
Oct. 17. 362 miles. Light NW wind. Small sea.
Oct. 18. 606 miles. Gentle W wind. Moderate sea.
Oct. 19. 611 miles. Moderate W'ly wind. Moderate sea.
Oct. 20. 601 miles. Strong W'ly wind. Rough head seas.
Oct. 21. 601 miles. Strong W'ly wind. Rough head seas.
To Ambrose 316 miles. Arrived at Ambrose Chan. Lt.V. 12:15 a.m., Oct. 22
Total distance 3097 miles.
Sea passage 5 days 7 hours 53 min.
Average speed 24.21 knots per hour.
—Captain H. Hatley, USNR, Commanding

AMERICA'S CUP CHALLENGES

1851—*America* (USA) defeated a British fleet to win the Hundred Guinea Cup
1870—*Magic* (USA) defeated *Cambria* (GB)
1871—*Columbia* and *Sappho* (USA) defeated *Livonia* (GB)
1876—*Madeleine* (USA) defeated *Countess of Dufferin* (Canada)
1881—*Mischief* (USA) defeated *Atalanta* (Canada)
1885—*Puritan* (USA) defeated *Genesta* (GB)
1886—*Mayflower* (USA) defeated *Galatea* (GB)
1887—*Volunteer* (USA) defeated *Thistle* (GB)
1893—*Vigilant* (USA) defeated *Valkyrie II* (GB)
1895—*Defender* (USA) defeated *Valkyrie III* (GB)
1899—*Columbia* (USA) defeated *Shamrock* (Ireland)
1901—*Columbia* (USA) defeated *Shamrock II* (Ireland)
1902—*Reliance* (USA) defeated *Shamrock III* (Ireland)
1920—*Resolute* (USA) defeated *Shamrock IV* (Ireland)
1930—*Enterprise* (USA) defeated *Shamrock V* (Ireland)
1934—*Rainbow* (USA) defeated *Endeavour* (GB)
1937—*Ranger* (USA) defeated *Endeavour II* (GB)
1958—*Columbia* (USA) defeated *Sceptre* (GB)
1962—*Weatherly* (USA) defeated *Gretel* (Australia)
1964—*Constellation* (USA) defeated *Sovereign* (GB)
1967—*Intrepid* (USA) defeated *Dame Pattie* (Australia)
1970—*Intrepid* (USA) defeated *Gretel II* (Australia)
1974—*Courageous* (USA) defeated *Southern Cross* (Australia)
1977—*Courageous* (USA) defeated *Australia* (Australia)
1980—*Freedom* (USA) defeated *Australia* (Australia)
1983—*Australia II* (Australia) defeated *Liberty* (USA)
1987—*Stars & Stripes* (USA) defeated *Kookaburra III* (Australia)
1988—*Stars & Stripes* (USA) defeated *New Zealand* (New Zealand)
1992—*America* (USA) defeated *Il Moro di Venezia* (Italy)
1995—*Black Magic* (New Zealand) defeated *Young America* (USA)
2000—*Black Magic* (New Zealand) defeated *Prada* (Italy)
2003—*Alinghi* (Switzerland) defeated *Team New Zealand* (New Zealand)

THE CREW ON A MODERN INTERNATIONAL AMERICA'S CUP CLASS YACHT

1 helmsman
1 tactician
1 navigator
1 mainsheet trimmer
2 headsail trimmers
5 winch grinders
1 spinnaker trimmer
1 sail packer/halyard man
1 foredeck hand
1 bowman
1 observer—owner, designer, or other supercargo

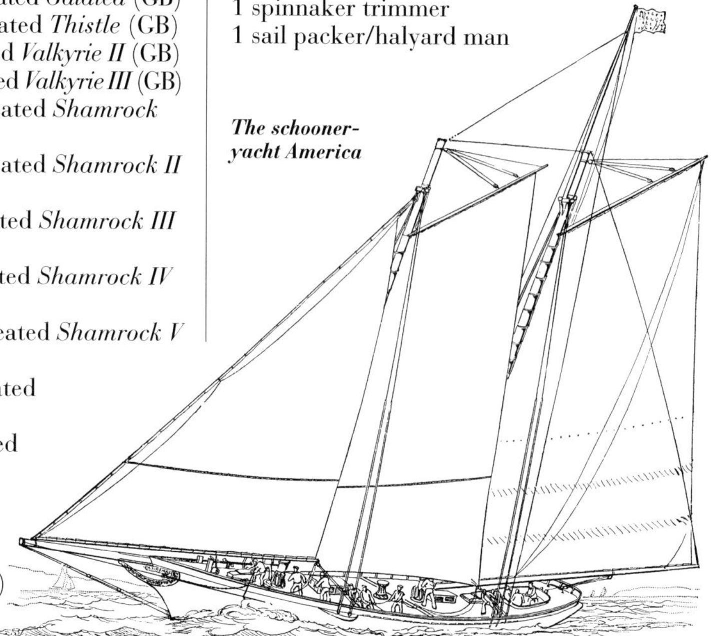

The schooner-yacht America

The America's Cup, yachting's great and garish grail, is a tumorous tureen no handsomer than a camel.
—Tom Callahan

OCTOBER

Monday
15

1881— *The American Angler*, the first American magazine devoted to the sport of fishing, began publication.

Tuesday
16

1899—For the first time, journalists used wireless telegraphy to report the progress of the America's Cup races, then held off New York City.

Wednesday
17

1840—The steamship *Arcadia* arrived in Boston Harbor, Massachusetts, after a passage of 12 days, 12 hours, from Liverpool, England, the shortest time to date.

Thursday
18

1853—The *David Crockett*, one of the longest lived (40 years) of the American clipper-ship fleet, was launched in Mystic, Connecticut.

Friday ◐
19

1774—In what came to be known as the Peggy Stewart Tea Party, citizens of Annapolis, Maryland, angered by British taxes, destroyed the English brig *Peggy Stewart* and her cargo of tea.

Saturday
20

1811—The *New Orleans*, the first steamboat on the Ohio and Mississippi Rivers, departed Pittsburgh on her maiden voyage.

Sunday
21

1871—The first official sailing-canoe race in the United States, sponsored by the New York Canoe Club, was held in Flushing Bay, New York.

THE SHIP *CARPATHIAN*, SOUTH PACIFIC OCEAN, WEST OF CHILE, OCTOBER 24, 1891

In the morning, at about 1 a.m., the man at the wheel saw smoke coming up the after cabin skylight, and called the attention of the second mate to it; the second then ran into the cabin and saw smoke coming up from the lazarette hatch. He called the captain, and told him there was fire down below. The captain called all hands on deck to pass water into the after cabin, but by the time they had opened the after hatch, they were driven out of the cabin by smoke. We tried to get water down the after hatch, but we found that the fire was too strong for us. The Captain then gave the order to get the boats out. We started with the port lifeboat; it was hauled forward and launched, but it sank right away; then we put the dinghy over, and three hands got into her: after that, the pinnace had some gear put into her and was launched; the gig was then put into the water. We then pulled clear of the ship; the pinnace tried to come alongside of the gig, but she sank, and the men all got into the gig. So there was only the gig and the dinghy afloat to carry 27 hands.

—a survivor

CONVERSATION BETWEEN NOAH AND A MODERN MARINE-SAFETY INSPECTOR IF THE ARK WERE TO BE BUILT IN OUR TIMES, IMAGINED BY MARK TWAIN

"Have any of you ever been to sea?"

"No, sir."

"Where were you reared?"

"On a farm—all of us."

"This vessel requires a crew of eight hundred men, she not being a steamer. You must provide them."

. . . .

"Who designed this vessel?"

"I did, sir."

"Is it your first attempt?"

"Yes, sir."

"I partly suspected it. Cargo?"

"Animals."

"Kind?"

"All kinds."

"Wild, or tame?"

"Mainly wild."

"Foreign or domestic?"

"Mainly foreign."

"Principal wild ones?"

"Megatherium, elephant, rhinoceros, lion, tiger, wolf, snakes—all the wild things of all climes—two of each."

"Securely caged?"

"No, not caged."

"They must have iron cages.... How many animals are there?"

"Big ones, seven thousand; big and little together, ninety-eight thousand."

"You must provide twelve hundred keepers."

REGULATIONS GOVERNING MINIMUM EQUIPMENT AND ACCOMMODATIONS STANDARDS

The safety of a yacht and her crew is the sole and inescapable responsibility of the owner, or owner's representative, the captain, who must do his best to ensure that the yacht is fully found, thoroughly seaworthy and manned by an experienced crew who are physically fit to face bad weather. He must be satisfied as to the soundness of the hull, spars, rigging, sails and all gear. He must ensure that all safety equipment is properly maintained and stowed and that the crew know where it is kept and how it is to be used.

—Offshore Racing Council

Adventure means risking something.
—Alain Gerbault

OCTOBER

Monday
22

1882—N. C. (Newell Convers) Wyeth, illustrator of such nautical classics as *Treasure Island*, *Kidnapped*, *Great Stories of the Sea & Ships*, and *Captain Hornblower*, was born in Needham, Massachusetts.

Tuesday
23

1877—In a development that would have a monumental effect on transportation, on land as well as at sea, a patent was granted to Nicolaus Otto, and Francis and William Crossley, for a gasoline engine.

Wednesday
24

1944—The U.S. submarine *Tang* sank in Formosa Strait (now Taiwan Strait) after a torpedo she fired accidentally circled around and struck her; 87 lives were lost.

Thursday
25

1960—The icebreaker *Eastwind* got underway from Boston, Massachusetts, on the first circumnavigation of the globe by a U.S. Coast Guard cutter.

Friday ○
26

1875—W. Lyman was awarded a patent for a forward-facing rowing mechanism that, when fitted to a rowboat, allowed rowers to see where they were going instead of where they had been.

Saturday
27

1922—A national day dedicated to the U.S. Navy, now known as Navy Day, was celebrated for the first time.

Sunday
28

1919—The U.S. Congress passed the Volstead Act over presidential veto, thus institutionalizing Prohibition and setting the stage for the Golden Era of rumrunning at sea.

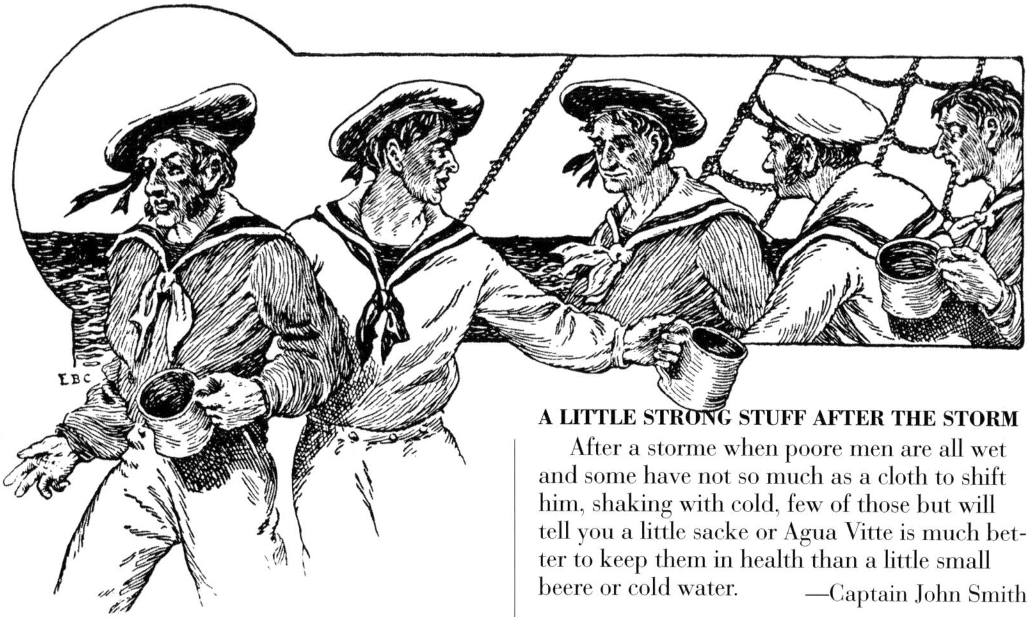

THE SPENDTHRIFT, DRUNKEN SAILOR DEFINED, IN A COMPLAINT BY CAPTAIN EDWARD WHEELER, R.N., TO HIS CREW (1760)

I have observed too, whenever ye get any money paid, ye do not act with it like rational creatures and lay it out on clothes and necessaries, but ye throw it immediately away on dirty whores and in stinking gin.

THE BRIG *THOMAS W. ROWLAND*, MOUTH OF THE MISSISSIPPI RIVER, NOVEMBER 3, 1856

This morning, the wind being favorable, we proceeded on up the river.... We soon came up to the English turn, and a crooked turn it is indeed. First we sail in one direction perhaps a mile, then in another, first north then nearly south, till we come in view of the tall steeples and masts of the ships at New Orleans. And at ten A.M. we were fairly up, and anchored a little below the shipping. At 4 a tow boat came alongside and took us to the Levee No. 23 and in the picayune tier opposite the market. Most of the sailor men have gone on shore, and probably some or all are by this time carrying a "brick in their hats," and thus find it rather difficult to navigate on the land. Foolish creatures, why will they treat themselves in the manner they do? It takes but a few days for them to rid themselves of their hard-earned money. Their first object generally is to go to some clothing store, and there get a whole new fit-out, then get drunk as soon as possible.

—Mary Rowland

A LITTLE STRONG STUFF AFTER THE STORM

After a storme when poore men are all wet and some have not so much as a cloth to shift him, shaking with cold, few of those but will tell you a little sacke or Agua Vitte is much better to keep them in health than a little small beere or cold water. —Captain John Smith

I drink to your charm, your beauty, and your brains—which gives you a rough idea of how hard up I am for a drink. —Groucho Marx

To make short this sad part of my story, we went the old way of all sailors, the punch was made, and I was made drunk with it.

—from *Robinson Crusoe*, by Daniel Defoe

One tequila, two tequila, three tequila, floor.

—George Carlin

GROG

Originally, grog was rum diluted with water. These days, it tends to be a little more elaborate:

LIME-DARK GROG

2 oz. dark rum
2 oz. water
1 tbsp. lime juice
1 tbsp. brown sugar
cloves and/or cinnamon stick to taste

Heat until the sugar dissolves and pour into a mug.

CITRUS GROG

1 oz. light rum
2 oz. dark rum
1 oz. lime juice
1 oz. grapefruit juice
1 tsp. powdered sugar

Poured all over ice, shake, and strain into tall glass.

At sea, or ashore, or when harbour'd,
The mariner's compass is grog.
—from an old sea song

OCT/NOV

Monday
29

1890—The steamer Vizcaya collided with the schooner *Cornelius Hargraves* off Barnegat Light, New Jersey, both vessels sinking in seven minutes; 70 lives were lost.

Tuesday
30

1992—Kenichi Horie departed Honolulu, Hawaii, for Okinawa, Japan, in a pedal boat, a distance of 4,660 miles (he arrived safely).

Wednesday
31 HALLOWEEN

1925—Harry Pidgeon returned to Los Angeles, California, in the 34-foot home-built yawl *Islander* following a solo circumnavigation of the globe, the second person to do so.

Thursday ◑
1

1898—The American Shipmasters' Association was renamed the American Bureau of Shipping.

Friday
2

1853—*Red Jacket*, one of the fastest of the clipper ships, was launched in Rockland, Maine.

Saturday
3

1918—The German naval fleet at Kiel mutinied, the first act leading to Germany's capitulation in World War I.

Sunday
4 DAYLIGHT SAVING ENDS

1984—The USCGC *Northwind*, seizing 20 tons of marijuana from a ship off Jamaica, became the first icebreaker to make a drug bust.

DIFFERENT TYPES OF LOG

Rough log—notations made as events take place; used in preparation of the smooth log

Smooth log—permanent record of the day's events, prepared by the mate for the captain

Official log—personnel record containing details about wages, fines, punishments, sicknesses, births, deaths, marriages, desertions, etc.

Abstract log—synopsis of a voyage

SCALE FOR LOGGING THE STATE OF THE SEA

0—calm, 0' in height
1—smooth, 1'
2—slight, 1–3'
3—moderate, 3–5'
4—rough, 5–8'
5—very rough, 8–12'
6—high, 12–20'
7—very high, 20–40'
8—mountainous, 40'-plus
9—confused

SCALE FOR LOGGING THE STATE OF THE SWELL

0—no swell
1—low, short or average length
2—low, long length
3—moderate, short length
4—moderate, average length
5—moderate, long length
6—heavy, short length
7—heavy, average length
8—heavy, long length
9—confused

SYMBOLS FOR LOGGING THE WEATHER, ONE OF SEVERAL SYSTEMS USED OVER THE YEARS

Clr—clear
Sct—scattered clouds
Bkn—broken clouds
Ovc—overcast
T—thunderstorm
R—rain
L—drizzle
E—sleet
F—fog
S—snow
A—hail
H—haze
K—smoke
D—dust

THE KETCH *SAOIRSE*, INDIAN OCEAN NEAR DURBAN, SOUTH AFRICA, NOVEMBER 9, 1923

Begins dull; air very wet. A short choppy sea stops the ship much, and she is making a lot of leeway; later sky clearing and wind more northerly. 10.30—Very light; set gaff-topsail. 11.30—Tacked; wind went round to S.W., very light; uncomfortable swell from N.E. and S.W. Noon.—No observation. Spoke whalers *Henkules* and *Edda*. P.M.—Wind freshening: in gaff-topsail. Observation puts us about 15 miles off shore; nothing visible through haze. At 13.30 gybed and altered course to east to get an offing. Thunder, lightning, and heavy squalls. In mizzen and 2 reefs in mainsail. Ends fine; wind light.

—Conor O'Brien

That the log should be written in seamanlike prose
Is a rule that every seafaring man knows.
—H. W. Tilman

NOVEMBER

Monday
5

1918—The former Cunard passenger liner *Campania*, converted by the Royal Navy to an aircraft carrier, dragged her anchors in the Firth of Forth, Scotland, collided with the battleship HMS *Revenge*, and sank.

Tuesday
6

1798—Horatio Nelson of the Royal Navy, in honor of his magnificent naval victory at Abukir Bay, Egypt, was given the title of Baron Nelson of the Nile.

Wednesday
7

1872—The hermaphrodite brig *Mary Celeste* sailed from New York, bound for Genoa, Italy; she was found a month later east of the Azores, sailing herself, her entire crew mysteriously gone.

Thursday
8

1859—In one of the more notable cases of unfortunately unfulfilled promise, Donald McKay, the clipper-ship designer and builder, wrote a prospectus for a book entitled *Theory and Practice of Naval Architecture*, which he never wrote.

Friday ●
9

1959—Charles Robert Patterson, marine artist, best known for his accuracy in the painting of sailing ships, died in New York City.

Saturday
10

1913—*Lightship No. 82*, stationed on Lake Erie near Buffalo, New York, sank during a storm; all six of the crew were lost.

Sunday
11

REMEMBRANCE SUNDAY / UK & CANADA
VETERANS DAY / US

1887—Construction of the Manchester Ship Canal, which would connect the inland city of Manchester, England, with the Irish Sea, got underway.

Eighty percent of rules of thumb only apply twenty percent of the time.

—anon.

RULES OF THUMB

Choosing a boat: a foot of waterline for every year of a person's age.

Boat size: each additional five feet of waterline length approximately doubles the cost of upkeep.

Time to build a boat: twice the best estimate.

Labor to build a boat: one quarter of an hour per pound of displacement.

Boatyard repairs: double cost estimates, quadruple time estimates.

Air-drying lumber: one year per inch of thickness.

Steam-bending wood: one hour per inch of thickness.

Painting and varnishing: two thin coats are better than one thick one.

Spars: carbon-fiber is generally 20 percent stiffer than the equivalent in aluminum.

Sail area, cruising boat: 100 square feet of sail for every ton of displacement.

Accommodations: neatness equals roominess.

Choosing an anchor: the heaviest you can physically handle.

Anchor scope: in normal conditions, seven feet of line for every foot of depth.

Docking lines per boat: two bow, two stern, two spring.

Length of bow and stern lines: two-thirds boat length.

Length of spring lines: full length of boat.

Useless rope: 50 percent of the visible strands have been worn to fuzz.

Knots: a rope with a knot in it has lost approximately half its strength.

Distance from a thunderstorm in miles: divide by five the number of seconds between seeing the lightning and hearing the thunder.

Endurance: swimming a quarter mile is approximately the same as running a mile.

Canoe paddle length, bow: distance from your chin to the ground.

Canoe paddle length, stern: distance from your eyes to the ground.

Oar length: twice the width of the thwart plus the freeboard at the position of the thwart.

Fuel required: one-third to get where you are going, one-third to get back, one-third in reserve.

Waves: generally, every seventh wave is larger than the preceding six.

DISTANCE OFF RULES OF THUMB—WHAT YOU CAN SEE IN CLEAR WEATHER

8 miles—tall buildings, lighthouses, etc.

4 miles—light-colored beach

3 miles—breakers at the horizon

2 miles—windows, large buoys

1½ miles—small buoys

1 mile—individual trees, color of large buoy, shape and color of small buoy, people as a black dot

1,200 feet—people's arms and legs

750 feet—people's faces

Rules of thumb are made to be broken.

—anon.

THE FOLDING KAYAK *LIBERIA III*, MID-ATLANTIC OCEAN, NOVEMBER 15, 1956

Slowly, slowly I paddled against the breath blowing against me from the west. The sea boasted a pretty shingled pattern; I did about one knot with my paddle. I tired quickly and rested often. Without warning, a shark appeared beside me. It was about nine feet long, the average size for a high-sea shark. It stared at me out of its round, pig eyes, so close I could have reached out and touched it. I found my camera and took pictures while the fish dawdled under and around the rubber canoe. I had time to get at my movie camera, because the shark continued circling around the air tubes, surrounded by a host of pilot fish. I was neither particularly eager to have a shark near me, nor very sure of how to get rid of it. Watching it closely until it came within reach, I hit it on the head with the paddle. My action had no effect whatsoever. After a while, however, it swam off, leaving me convinced that it had no bad intentions toward me. It behaved as a zoologist would have expected.

—Dr. Hannes Lindemann

I never was on the dull, tame shore,
But I loved the great sea more and more.
—Brian Waller Procter

NOVEMBER

Monday
12 VETERANS DAY OBSERVED

1965—The passenger ship *Yarmouth Castle* caught fire and sank between Florida and the Bahamas; 87 lives were lost.

Tuesday
13

1927—The Holland Tunnel under the Hudson River, linking New York City and New Jersey, was opened to traffic.

Wednesday
14

1909—Joshua Slocum, the first person to sail around the world singlehanded, was declared legally dead after presumably being lost at sea. (This is the date on which he last set sail.)

Thursday
15

1904—A contract for the construction of the first eight sailing yachts of the New York Thirty class was signed between the New York Yacht Club and the Herreshoff Manufacturing Co.

Friday
16

1993—Tim Severin and crew, crossing the Pacific eastward from Hong Kong to prove Asians could have made the voyage centuries earlier, abandoned the bamboo raft *Hsu Fu* 1,000 miles from North America; all were rescued.

Saturday ◐
17

1875—The Thames Rule was adopted for measurement by the Yacht Racing Association of Britain.

Sunday
18

1875—The schooner *Sunshine* stranded near Cape Foulweather, Oregon; 20 lives were lost.

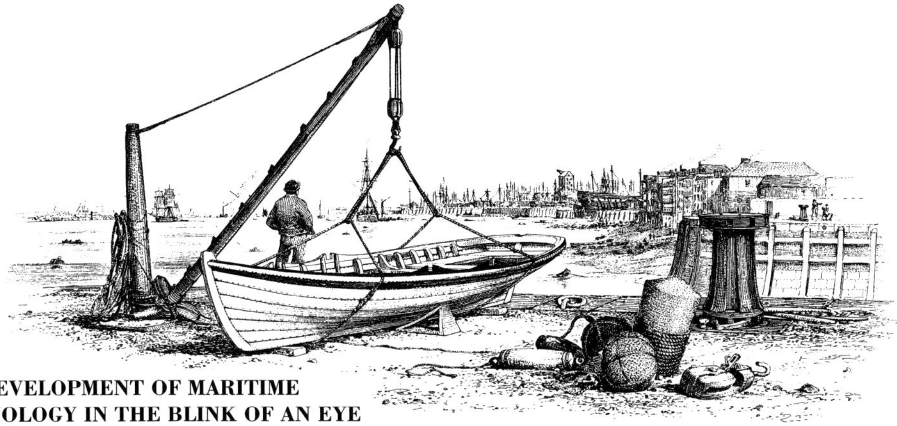

THE DEVELOPMENT OF MARITIME TECHNOLOGY IN THE BLINK OF AN EYE

3000 BC—Oar-powered galleys with one tier of oarsmen in use in Mediterranean Sea.
8th century BC—Biremes, two-tiered galleys, in use in Mediterranean Sea.
5th century BC—Triremes, three-tiered galleys, in use in Mediterranean Sea.
4th century AD—Lateen sails became more common than square sails in the Mediterranean Sea.
9th century—Viking ship developed in Scandinavia.
12th century—Compass in use in Europe.
13th century—Caravel began evolution in southern Europe.
13th century—Cross staff in use for measuring celestial altitudes in navigation.
13th century—Stern-mounted rudder began to supplant side-mounted steering oar in northern Europe.
14th century—Naval guns in use aboard ship.
15th century—Quadrant in use by Portuguese for measuring celestial altitudes in navigation.
16th century—Galleon began evolution.
1757—Sextant, for measuring celestial altitudes in navigation, invented.
1759—First real chronometer, for determining longitude at sea, built.
1801—A steam-powered tugboat towed two barges for 20 miles, in Scotland.
1807—First successful commercial steamboat service began, on the Hudson River.
1819—First steam-powered vessel crossed the Atlantic Ocean.
1821—First seagoing iron-hull vessel launched.
1832—Transatlantic steam-powered packet service established.
1837—Morse code developed.
mid-19th century—Clipper ships developed.
1854—Breech-loading, rifled naval gun invented.
1859—First ironclad warship launched in France.
1864—Self-propelled torpedo invented.
1869—Suez Canal opened.
1876—Plimsoll lines, indicating safe loading for merchant vessels, adopted by Britain.
1879—Electric lights first used in a passenger ship.
1900—First fully operational naval submarine built.
1902—First ship fitted with wireless telegraph.
1910—First aircraft launched from a ship.
1914—Panama Canal opened.
1930s—Radar developed.
1940s—Loran developed.
1954—First nuclear-powered vessel, a submarine, launched.
1985—GPS made available to the public.

THE CRUISING CUTTER *CALTHA*, PALMA DE MALLORCA, MEDITERRANEAN SEA, NOVEMBER 22, 1921

It was dark when we rounded Cape Cala Figuera and headed up Palma Bay. Then a breeze came, and it came ahead. So, after all, we were forced to beat, even to the last inch. It was a very dark night, and the breeze served us well; we watched the city spreading out and growing more distinct as we drew nearer. Porto Pi light appeared a miserable affair, but welcome—and soon afterwards the occulting light on the breakwater, very hard to distinguish from the shore lights because of the mirage, which raised them all up and magnified them grotesquely. When we were three miles away we could see lights in houses, and the street lamps, shining on up the buildings near them. We heard trolley cars grinding on the curves, and the occasional hoot of an automobile horn. We came gliding in, very still, watching the black masts of all the ships against the sky, and the restless reflections of the lights in the glassy water.

—Arthur Sturges Hildebrand

The sea is the great maker of men.
—Basil Lubbock

NOVEMBER

Monday
19

1889—E. F. Knight arrived off Trinidad Island in the South Atlantic to search for buried treasure. The search was unsuccessful, but Knight's chronicle of his adventures, *The Cruise of the Alerte*, became a bestseller.

Tuesday
20

1881—Captain Paul Boyton, in a rubber suit, arrived in St. Louis, Missouri, at the end of a 3,500-mile swim down the Missouri River from Montana; he wrote about his exploits in the book *Roughing It In Rubber* (1886).

Wednesday
21

1991—Gerard d'Aboville arrived at Ilwaco, Washington, in the rowboat *Sector* at the end of the first west-to-east singlehanded crossing of the Pacific Ocean under oars.

Thursday
22

THANKSGIVING / US

1808—Thomas Cook, who made his fortune booking travel excursions, most by steamship and railroad, was born in Melbourne, Derbyshire, England.

Friday
23

1869—The tea clipper *Cutty Sark*, whose name is Gaelic for torn (or short) shirt, was launched in Dumbarton, Scotland. She is preserved to this day in Greenwich, England.

Saturday ○
24

1922—Robert Erskine Childers, author of *The Riddle of the Sands* and a member of the IRA, was executed by the Irish Free State for gun-running.

Sunday
25

1842—Thomas Buttersworth, marine artist, died in Greenwich, England.

THE MASSACHUSETTS PRIVATEER BRIG *TYRANNICIDE*, ATLANTIC OCEAN EAST OF THE WINDWARD ISLES, NOVEMBER 27, 1776

7 [a.m.] Saw a sail to the westward gave chase, saw another to the Northward at 10 came up with them both they laying too for us received a broad Side from the Bark *John*, gave her a shot, she struck, gave the other Ship a Shot, she struck, sent the boat on board both of them.

1 [p.m.] Found the Bark to be from London Wm Barrass Master for Antagua & the Ship from East Florida for Granada James Crichton Master.

6 [p.m.] Mannd the Bark and sent away for Salem, the Ship in Company.

—Captain John Fisk

There are few undertakings that will keep a man happily at home more than model making, and certainly there are few that will give him a better understanding of ship construction and the history of naval architecture, and none that will give him a higher appreciation of workmanship. —L. Francis Herreshoff

WORDS TO MODEL BY, FROM HOWARD I. CHAPELLE

Accuracy in a model is of far more importance in giving a model value than fine workmanship alone. Actually, of course, the two should go together, but there are many well-made models built to poor plans or none at all which represent nothing more than a complete waste of time, materials and labor.

THE THREE BASIC WAYS TO BUILD A HULL FOR A SHIP MODEL

Carve it from a block of wood, either built-up or solid.
Plank it over bulkheads or a framework.
Make a plug, then a mold, and lay it up with fiberglass.

THE IDEAL WOOD FOR MODEL MAKING

Seasoned and stable
Not liable to splitting, twisting, or warping
Soft enough to work but hard enough to hold an edge
Bendable
Fine, close grain
Neutral in color if to be stained
Accepts glue, paint, and other finishes readily

WOOD STOCK FOR MODEL MAKING

Alder—frames, planks, fittings, spars
Apple, crab apple—frames, planks, fittings
Bamboo—dowels, trunnels
Basswood (aka limewood)—carved hulls, deck structures
Birch—frames, planks, deck structures
Boxwood—all parts of model; especially good for fittings
Cedar—carved hulls, half hulls, planking
Cherry—frames, planks, fittings, spars
Cocobolo—deadeyes, blocks, hearts
Dogwood—fittings
Ebony—wales, rails, bulwarks, fittings
Elm—backbone, frames, knees
Holly—planks, fittings
Hophornbeam—fittings
Hornbeam—fittings
Ironwood—fittings
Mahogany (Honduras)—carved hulls and half hulls
Maple—bases, cases, fittings, frames, planks
Mountain ash—frames, planks, fittings
Pear—fittings, planks, frames
Pine—carved hulls, half hulls
Poplar—frames, carved hulls, half hulls, bases, cases
Rosewood—fittings
Spruce—spars
Sycamore—planks
Walnut—bases, cases, carved hulls, half hulls

Of all man's creations there is nothing more beautiful, I think, than a good-looking sailboat under sail.
—Francis S. Kinney

NOV/DEC

Monday
26

1999—The passenger ferry *Sleipner*, a catamaran, sank at the mouth of the Boemla Fjord, Norway; 16 lives were lost.

Tuesday
27

1889—The Maryland schooner *Lawson*, dredging illegally for oysters in Virginia waters, was run down and sunk by the Virginia police boat *Augustus* off Hog Island, Chesapeake Bay.

Wednesday
28

1859—Washington Irving, author of *The Life and Voyages of Christopher Columbus*, died in Tarrytown, New York.

Thursday
29

1520—Ferdinand Magellan's fleet sailed into the Pacific Ocean after having passed through the body of water between South America and Tierra del Fuego that was then known as the Strait of the Eleven Thousand Virgins; it's now called the Strait of Magellan.

Friday
30

1819—Cyrus Field, builder of the underwater transatlantic telegraph cable, was born in Stockbridge, Massachusetts.

Saturday ◑
1

1979—The volume of plastic produced in the United States exceeded for the first time that of steel, thus solidifying the hegemony of the fiberglass boat.

Sunday
2

1905—The keel of HMS *Dreadnought*, the first modern (or all-big-gun) battleship, was laid in Portsmouth, England.

NAVY PERSONNEL, CONTEMPORARY SLANG (U.S. NAVY, UNLESS INDICATED OTHERWISE)

Airdale; also brownshoe; also suck-and-blow sailor; also airy-fairy (RN); also wafoo (RN)—naval aviator
Amp tramp (RCN)—ship's electrician
Anchor clanker; also deck ape; also boats—boatswain's mate
Beagle (RN)—wardroom steward
Bilge rat; also stoker, stokes (RN)—member of black gang or A-gang
Black gang; also snipes—engineroom crew
Brass—officers
Bubblehead; also deeps (RN)—submariner; also diver
Bull ensign—senior ensign
Bunting tosser; also flag wagger; also skivvy waver; also bunts (RN)—signalman
Buoy jumper—deck ape who leaps from the ship to a mooring buoy to handle mooring lines
Cannon cocker; also gun buster (RCN)—gunner
Charlie Oscar; also old man—commanding officer
Cheng—chief engineer
Chips—ship's carpenter
Chop; also pork chop, pusser (RN)—supply officer
Clanky (RN)—mechanical engineer
Crippie—cryptographer
Dicksmith; also pecker checker, dick doc, chancre mechanic, penis machinist—navy doctor or corpsman
Fang bosun; also farrier—dentist
Grunt; also leatherneck, gyrene, jarhead, mud puppy, bootneck (RN), jolly (RN)—a marine
Jack (RN); also whitehat, raghat, squid, swinging dick—sailor
Killick (RN, RCN)—leading man
Messcrank; also crank, scullery slut (RCN)—food-service worker (waiter, busboy, pot washer, potato peeler, etc.)
Mustang—commissioned officer who worked his way up from enlisted ranks
O-ganger; also zero—officer
Paybob (RN)—supply officer
Ping jockey—sonarman
Sin bosun; also sky bosun, God botherer—chaplain
6 Ds—deep-diving death-defying denizens of the deep; i.e., submariners
Stew burner; also cooky, sloshy (RN)—cook
Turd herders—sewage-plant crew
Whitehat; also raghat—Enlisted personnel (E-1 through E-6)

THE 14-FOOT PAPER CANOE *MARIA THERESA*, ELIZABETH RIVER, VIRGINIA, DECEMBER 5, 1874

About noon I arrived at the locks of the Albemarle and Chesapeake Canal. The telegraph operator greeted me with the news that the company's agent in Norfolk had telegraphed to the lock-master to pass the paper canoe through with the freedom of the canal—the first honor of the kind that had fallen to my lot. The tide rises and falls at the locks in the river about three feet and a half. When I passed through, the difference in the level between the ends of the locks did not reach two feet.

—Nathaniel H. Bishop

Sea English is an old dialect.
—Joanna Carver Colcord

DECEMBER

Monday
3

1868—The clipper ship *Young America* was dismasted in a pampero off the Rio de la Plata, South Atlantic Ocean; she nevertheless continued on under jury rig around Cape Horn to San Francisco.

Tuesday
4

1915—Rear Admiral Frank Friday Fletcher became the first admiral of the U.S. Navy to be awarded the Congressional Medal of Honor, for heroism during the Battle of Veracruz, Mexico.

Wednesday
5 FIRST DAY OF HANUKKAH

1926—Sergei M. Eisenstein's movie *The Battleship Potemkin*, a dramatization of the mutiny aboard a Russian battleship during the 1905 revolution, made its debut.

Thursday
6

1817—Captain William Bligh, Royal Navy, victim of two mutinies, the most famous being that of HMS *Bounty*, died in London, England.

Friday
7

1942—Yeoman third class Dorothy Edith Lorne Tuttle became the first enlistee in the SPARS, the newly established women's branch of the U.S. Coast Guard.

Saturday
8

1846—The U.S. Navy brig *Somers* capsized and sank in a squall while chasing a blockade runner off Veracruz, Mexico; 32 lives were lost.

Sunday ●
9

1941—Germany began submarine warfare against U.S. shipping.

HEED THE SKY, HEED THE GLASS, SAYS FRANK COWPER

There are numerous wise saws about the weather, and how to tell it. For our part we have come to the conclusion that the weather-glass [barometer] and the sky are the best aids for forecasting the future. The weather-glass, by itself, we have known at fault, and the sky by itself has often misled us, but the two together, either corroborating or correcting, have seldom put us far wrong.

THINKING ABOUT THE YACHT *BILLY BABY*, LONDON, ENGLAND, DECEMBER 15, 1874

The *Billy Baby* is at last laid up for the winter, dismantled of all her gear, with her mast painted, two coats of varnish on her deck, and Ned [paid hand] in charge till I can so far emancipate myself as to return to her—to my real home, where alone I feel as though I belonged more or less to myself. Ned writes me the most delicious letters, in which he mixes the weather, the stores, the casualties at Shoreham, the desire he has to spend his first Christmas since fifteen years at home, and the breaking of two bottles of wine, in the most approved literary manner. Bill [paid hand] has returned to his mama, and is probably now on his way to the Dogger Bank for a course of fishing. Tom [paid hand] has also gone on the same business, and without coming to see me in London, which he was afraid to for fear of being run over in the streets. This delights me as being another proof that we only really fear that with which we are not acquainted.

—Thomas Gibson Bowles

A MEASURE OF SEA CONDITIONS—AKA THE BEERFORT WIND SCALE

Force 0: Sails hanging limp. Tiller tends itself.

Force 1: Beginning pressure on sails. If sheet is eased out, the tiller still tends itself.

Force 2: Sails flapping in the breeze, and boat drifting sideways to leeward. Sheets must be tightened and one hand put on the tiller. As the wind fills the sails, the boat heels. Case of beer must be placed on cockpit floor.

Force 3: The beer may be knocked over and must be supported or held in hand.

Force 4: Empty bottles rolling against each other on cockpit floor, must be thrown over the side.

Force 5: All beer streaming behind boat must be hauled in.

Force 6: Nobody can hold onto more than one beer at a time.

Force 7: The case of beer slides back and forth on cockpit floor. One person must be appointed to sit on it.

Force 8: Bottles can still be opened by one person. Beginning of difficulties pouring into the mouth without spilling.

Force 9: Bottle must be held with two hands. Only experts can get the cap off by themselves.

Force 10: Two people required to open bottles. Empties must be thrown to leeward only. Very difficult to find mouth. Some teeth may be knocked loose.

Force 11: The beer tends to foam out of bottle. Very difficult to drink. Lips split and teeth fall out.

Force 12: All open bottles foam. Impossible to drink. Temporary abstinence may be required.

—anon. (courtesy of the World Wide Web)

The pessimist complains about the wind;
the optimist expects it to change;
the realist adjusts the sails.
—William Arthur Ward

DECEMBER

Monday
10

1850—The steamship *City of Glasgow* departed Liverpool, England, inaugurating regular transatlantic service to Philadelphia, Pennsylvania, by the Inman Line.

Tuesday
11

1905—*Light Vessel No. 58*, on station off Nantucket Island, Massachusetts, developed an uncontrollable leak and sank; the crew was rescued by the lighthouse tender *Azalea.*

Wednesday
12

1869—Winfield M. [Martin] Thompson, sailor, journalist, author of *The Lawson History of the America's Cup*, was born in Southport, Maine.

Thursday
13

1577—Francis Drake departed Plymouth, England, in the *Pelican*, soon to be renamed the *Golden Hind*, on a voyage around the world.

Friday
14

1844—The steamboat *Belle of Clarksville* was run down and sunk by the steamboat *Louisiana* on the Mississippi River; more than 30 people drowned.

Saturday
15

1976—The tanker *Argo Merchant* ran aground on a shoal near Nantucket Island, spilling 7.7 million gallons of crude oil.

Sunday
16

1917—The U.S. submarine *F1* sank after colliding with the submarine *F3* off San Diego, California; 19 lives were lost.

THE LASS THAT LOVES A SAILOR
by Charles Dibdin

The moon on the ocean
Was dimmed by a ripple
Affording a chequered delight;
The gay jolly tars
Passed a word for the tipple,
And the toast—
For 'twas Saturday night:
Some sweetheart or wife
He loved as his life
Each drank, and wished
He could hail her:
But the standing toast
That pleased the most,
Was "The wind that blows,
The Ship that goes,
And the lass that loves a sailor!"

Some drank "The Queen,"
And some her brave ships,
And some "The Constitution";
Some "May our foes,
And all such rips,
Yield to English resolution!"
That fate might bless
Some Poll or Bess,
And that they soon
Might hail her:
But the standing toast
That pleased the most,
Was "The wind that blows,
The Ship that goes,
And the lass that loves a sailor!"

Some drank "The Prince,"
And some "Our Land,"
This glorious land of freedom!
Some that our tars
May never stand
For heroes brave to lead them!
That she who's in distress may find,
Such friends as ne'er will fail her.
But the standing toast
That pleased the most,
Was "The wind that blows,
The Ship that goes,
And the lass that loves a sailor!"

THE QUAHOG SKIFF *BUGSY'S BOOMER*, OYSTER RIVER, CHATHAM, MASSACHUSETTS, DECEMBER 23, 1956

We took her out for a spin for the last time before the holidays. The tide was right so Fred said let's run out to Monomoy and poach some black ducks for Christmas dinner but once we got outside the wind was wrong—against the tide and throwing up whitecaps and no end of spray—so we ran into the river to see what we could see. Great idea, dumb consequences. We were halfway up the river just after the first big bend when three ducks flew out of a small bog near the shore about five o'clock toward twelve, in other words along our right side, real low. Fred jumped up and fired both barrels, missed the first bird, got the second. Then when we went to pick it up Fred slipped (ice on the floorboards) and fell in. By the time we got back it was hard to tell which was more frozen, Fred or the duck.

—E. H. Morgan

CHARLES DIBDIN, COMPOSER

One of the most successful composers of sea songs, Charles Dibdin nevertheless had hardly any actual seagoing experience. His only shipboard time was as a passenger on a ship bound from England for India that had to return home after a short time at sea due to storm damage. The son of a silversmith, he was born near Southampton, England, on March 15, 1745. As a young boy he studied music at Winchester Cathedral and then, at age fifteen, went to London and became a singing actor. His first work as a composer was an operetta produced at Covent Garden; for years he was connected with Drury Lane, both as an actor and as a composer. Dibdin's sea songs, most of which were written on King's commission and were patriotic in nature, were said to be worth 10,000 sailors to the English cause during wartime, especially during the American revolutionary war. During Dibdin's professional career, he wrote more than 1,300 songs of all types, many of which were the most popular of their time, though now those most associated with him are the sea songs.

If Winter comes, can Spring be far behind?
—Percy Bysshe Shelley

DECEMBER

Monday ◐
17

1866—A tunnel from Chicago two miles out into Lake Michigan was completed. The first of its kind, it was designed to supply the city with drinking water.

Tuesday
18

1944—During a typhoon off the Philippines, three U.S. Navy destroyers—*Hull, Spence,* and *Monaghan*—capsized and sank, and at least 28 other vessels were damaged; nearly 800 lives were lost.

Wednesday
19

1851—J. M. W. Turner, artist, painter of ships and seascapes, died in Chelsea, London, England.

Thursday
20

1987—The passenger ferry *Doña Paz* and the oil tanker Vector collided, burned, and sank in Tablas Strait, Philippines; more than 4,000 lives were lost.

Friday
21

1936—By Executive Order, the U.S. Coast Guard was assigned icebreaking duty.

Saturday
22 WINTER SOLSTICE

1963—The cruise ship *Lakonia*, 180 miles north of the island of Madeira, caught fire and burned; 128 lives were lost.

Sunday
23

1934—Japan renounced the Washington Naval Treaty of 1922 and the London Naval Treaty of 1930.

THE WHALESHIP *TIGER*, ATLANTIC OCEAN, JUST SOUTH OF THE EQUATOR, DECEMBER 26, 1845

Took the trade winds to day and I can with heartfelt satisfaction bid the calms farewell for ever. We shall soon rapidly recede from our native land which should I live cannot expect to see short of two years. When first out a lonesome sensation came over my mind when as the days passed I knew we were gliding farther and yet farther from land. But now I have no such feelings rather the reverse waft us on ye winds and bear us far away from home and kindred. I am with My Husband and by him will remain. No seas can now Divide us. He can have no trouble no sorrow but what I can know and share. When perplexed with the duties of the ship and those with whom he is connected I can soothe all ruffled feelings take up much of his attention and mind. If sick no hand like mine can soothe the sad heart and administer to his wishes. I am confident. Let what come I shall never regret coming on voyage with My Dear Companion's society also with the conviction in coming I did perfectly right.

—Mary Brewster, wife of the captain

Oh, have you heard the news, me Johnny?
One more day
We're homeward bound tomorrow
One more day
Only one more day, me Johnny
One more day
Oh, rock and roll me over
One more day

—from an old chantey

A LANDFALL IS A LANDFALL IS A LANDFALL

The steamer—which, with its machinery on deck, looked, as it worked its long slim legs, like some enormously magnified insect or antediluvian monster—dashed at great speed up a beautiful bay; and presently they saw some heights, and islands, and a long, flat, straggling city.

"And this," said Mr Tapley, looking far ahead, "is the Land of Liberty, is it? Very well. I'm agreeable. Any land will do for me, after so much water!"

—from *Martin Chuzzlewit*, by Charles Dickens

I saw three ships come sailing by,
Come sailing by, come sailing by,
I saw three ships come sailing by,
On Christmas Day in the morning.

—anon.

ONCE A SEAMAN, ALWAYS A SEAMAN

Men go to sea, before they know the unhappiness of that way of life; and when they have come to know it, they cannot escape from it, because it is then too late to choose another profession; as indeed is generally the case, with men, when they have once engaged in a particular way of life.

—from *The Life of Johnson*, by James Boswell

A good landfall always puts a navigator in a fine humor.
—Thomas Fleming Day

DECEMBER

Monday ○
24 CHRISTMAS EVE

1898—The first ship-to-shore wireless message was sent from the East Goodwin Lightship, in the English Channel, to the South Foreland Lighthouse, near Dover, England.

Tuesday
25 CHRISTMAS DAY

1857—The crew aboard the New Bedford whaleship *Junior*, in the Pacific Ocean, mutinied; the captain and third mate were murdered, the first and second mates were wounded.

Wednesday
26 FIRST DAY OF KWANZAA
BOXING DAY / UK & CANADA

1945—The first annual Sydney-to-Hobart Race, from Australia to Tasmania, got underway.

Thursday
27

1902—George Waters, the inventor of the paper boat, died in Troy, New York.

Friday
28

1838—Britain's Lords of the Admiralty adopted the Beaufort Scale for recording the state of the wind and waves aboard ships of the Royal Navy.

Saturday
29

1938—Construction began on a floating bridge across Lake Washington, Seattle, Washington.

Sunday
30

1865—Rudyard Kipling, author of *Captains Courageous* and *The Seven Seas*, was born in Bombay, India.

COMING HOME

"Stand by to take in the tow-boat's line," said the mate.

"Stand by to take in the tow-boat's line, it is, sir," said the hands.

"Stand by with the cork fenders, lest the wharf shall scar her sides," said the mate.

"Stand by with the cork fenders, it is, sir," said the hands.

From ashore, from behind a warped gateway, a woman waved a shawl....

—Bill Adams

THE U.S. FRIGATE *CONSTELLATION*, ATLANTIC OCEAN WEST OF THE CANARY ISLANDS, JANUARY 5, 1800

Light airs and a heavy Swell from the Southward. The Store Ship about one mile Distance. The numerous colds & coughs with which the crew were effected, for a considerable time before we sailed from the Chesapeake begin to subside fast and by the Surgeons Report this day only ten remained in his list, and six of these are under Venereal complaints, of long standing, thus we may call the Ship Remarkably healthy. Employed repairing of Sails, that have been much injured by rats—and unhanging the port lids, as I find the Ship very Stiff in comparison to what she was with the 24 pd cannon on her decks—and these lids with their hinges & iron work, I calculate to average each 4 Cwt which takes from the Sides of the ship Six tons weight.

—Captain Thomas Truxton

HOME FROM THE SEA

We are strong and healthy, our arms feel possessed of sinews of whip-cord, we walk with an easy swing, and life flows joyously in our veins.

—Frank Cowper

Shipmates I'll bid you adieu
No more to sea will I go along with you
But to ramble this country through and through
And I'll be a ramblin' sailor

—from an old chantey

When first for shore
I left my shipping, I was will'd to take
A naval oar in hand, and with it make
My passage forth till such strange men I met
As knew no sea, nor ever salt did eat
With any victuals, who the purple beaks
Of ships did never see, nor that which breaks
The waves in curls, which is a fan-like oar,
And serves as wings with which a ship doth soar.
To let me know then when I was arrived
On that strange earth where such a people lived,
He gave me this for an unfailing sign:
When any one that took that oar of mine,
Borne on my shoulder, for a corn-cleanse fan,
I met ashore, and show'd to be a man
Of that land labour, there had I command
To fix mine oar.

—*The Odysseys of Homer*, translated by George Chapman

Ther ys no moe to saie.

—Geoffrey Chaucer

Then did I sudden understand
The sobbing of the sea.
—Frank Dempster Sherman

DEC/JAN

Monday ◑
31 NEW YEAR'S EVE

1980—The Loran-A navigation system, established during World War II, was discontinued.

Tuesday
1 NEW YEAR'S DAY

1984—The Fédération Internationale des Sociétés d'Aviron (FISA), the world governing body for competition rowing, banned the use of sliding riggers on racing shells; only sliding seats would be allowed.

Wednesday
2

1997—The Russian tanker *Nakhodka*, carrying five million gallons of oil, broke in two 90 miles off the coast of Japan; five days later, the bow of the ship ran aground 110 miles northwest of Tokyo.

Thursday
3

1877—The extreme clipper ship *Champion of the Seas*, carrying a cargo of guano, sprang a leak off Cape Horn and was abandoned; the crew was saved by the British bark *Windsor*.

Friday
4

1853—On a trial run, the experimental caloric vessel *Ericsson*—that is, a ship powered by heat—designed and built by Captain John Ericsson, proceeded down New York Harbor at 14 mph.

Saturday
5

1776—The first squadron of the Continental Navy was ordered to sea.

Sunday
6

1839—A two-day storm, the legendary "Big Wind," struck the coast of England and Ireland, causing extraordinary damage to shipping and shore structures.

2007

January

S	M	T	W	T	F	S
	1	2	3	4	5	6
7	8	9	10	11	12	13
14	15	16	17	18	19	20
21	22	23	24	25	26	27
28	29	30	31			

February

S	M	T	W	T	F	S
				1	2	3
4	5	6	7	8	9	10
11	12	13	14	15	16	17
18	19	20	21	22	23	24
25	26	27	28			

March

S	M	T	W	T	F	S
				1	2	3
4	5	6	7	8	9	10
11	12	13	14	15	16	17
18	19	20	21	22	23	24
25	26	27	28	29	30	31

April

S	M	T	W	T	F	S
1	2	3	4	5	6	7
8	9	10	11	12	13	14
15	16	17	18	19	20	21
22	23	24	25	26	27	28
29	30					

May

S	M	T	W	T	F	S
		1	2	3	4	5
6	7	8	9	10	11	12
13	14	15	16	17	18	19
20	21	22	23	24	25	26
27	28	29	30	31		

June

S	M	T	W	T	F	S
					1	2
3	4	5	6	7	8	9
10	11	12	13	14	15	16
17	18	19	20	21	22	23
24	25	26	27	28	29	30

July

S	M	T	W	T	F	S
1	2	3	4	5	6	7
8	9	10	11	12	13	14
15	16	17	18	19	20	21
22	23	24	25	26	27	28
29	30	31				

August

S	M	T	W	T	F	S
			1	2	3	4
5	6	7	8	9	10	11
12	13	14	15	16	17	18
19	20	21	22	23	24	25
26	27	28	29	30	31	

September

S	M	T	W	T	F	S
						1
2	3	4	5	6	7	8
9	10	11	12	13	14	15
16	17	18	19	20	21	22
23	24	25	26	27	28	29
30						

October

S	M	T	W	T	F	S
	1	2	3	4	5	6
7	8	9	10	11	12	13
14	15	16	17	18	19	20
21	22	23	24	25	26	27
28	29	30	31			

November

S	M	T	W	T	F	S
				1	2	3
4	5	6	7	8	9	10
11	12	13	14	15	16	17
18	19	20	21	22	23	24
25	26	27	28	29	30	

December

S	M	T	W	T	F	S
						1
2	3	4	5	6	7	8
9	10	11	12	13	14	15
16	17	18	19	20	21	22
23	24	25	26	27	28	29
30	31					

2006

January

S	M	T	W	T	F	S
1	2	3	4	5	6	7
8	9	10	11	12	13	14
15	16	17	18	19	20	21
22	23	24	25	26	27	28
29	30	31				

February

S	M	T	W	T	F	S
			1	2	3	4
5	6	7	8	9	10	11
12	13	14	15	16	17	18
19	20	21	22	23	24	25
26	27	28				

March

S	M	T	W	T	F	S
			1	2	3	4
5	6	7	8	9	10	11
12	13	14	15	16	17	18
19	20	21	22	23	24	25
26	27	28	29	30	31	

April

S	M	T	W	T	F	S
						1
2	3	4	5	6	7	8
9	10	11	12	13	14	15
16	17	18	19	20	21	22
23	24	25	26	27	28	29
30						

May

S	M	T	W	T	F	S
	1	2	3	4	5	6
7	8	9	10	11	12	13
14	15	16	17	18	19	20
21	22	23	24	25	26	27
28	29	30	31			

June

S	M	T	W	T	F	S
				1	2	3
4	5	6	7	8	9	10
11	12	13	14	15	16	17
18	19	20	21	22	23	24
25	26	27	28	29	30	

July

S	M	T	W	T	F	S
						1
2	3	4	5	6	7	8
9	10	11	12	13	14	15
16	17	18	19	20	21	22
23	24	25	26	27	28	29
30	31					

August

S	M	T	W	T	F	S
		1	2	3	4	5
6	7	8	9	10	11	12
13	14	15	16	17	18	19
20	21	22	23	24	25	26
27	28	29	30	31		

September

S	M	T	W	T	F	S
					1	2
3	4	5	6	7	8	9
10	11	12	13	14	15	16
17	18	19	20	21	22	23
24	25	26	27	28	29	30

October

S	M	T	W	T	F	S
1	2	3	4	5	6	7
8	9	10	11	12	13	14
15	16	17	18	19	20	21
22	23	24	25	26	27	28
29	30	31				

November

S	M	T	W	T	F	S
			1	2	3	4
5	6	7	8	9	10	11
12	13	14	15	16	17	18
19	20	21	22	23	24	25
26	27	28	29	30		

December

S	M	T	W	T	F	S
					1	2
3	4	5	6	7	8	9
10	11	12	13	14	15	16
17	18	19	20	21	22	23
24	25	26	27	28	29	30
31						

2008

January

S	M	T	W	T	F	S
		1	2	3	4	5
6	7	8	9	10	11	12
13	14	15	16	17	18	19
20	21	22	23	24	25	26
27	28	29	30	31		

February

S	M	T	W	T	F	S
					1	2
3	4	5	6	7	8	9
10	11	12	13	14	15	16
17	18	19	20	21	22	23
24	25	26	27	28	29	

March

S	M	T	W	T	F	S
						1
2	3	4	5	6	7	8
9	10	11	12	13	14	15
16	17	18	19	20	21	22
23	24	25	26	27	28	29
30	31					

April

S	M	T	W	T	F	S
		1	2	3	4	5
6	7	8	9	10	11	12
13	14	15	16	17	18	19
20	21	22	23	24	25	26
27	28	29	30			

May

S	M	T	W	T	F	S
				1	2	3
4	5	6	7	8	9	10
11	12	13	14	15	16	17
18	19	20	21	22	23	24
25	26	27	28	29	30	31

June

S	M	T	W	T	F	S
1	2	3	4	5	6	7
8	9	10	11	12	13	14
15	16	17	18	19	20	21
22	23	24	25	26	27	28
29	30					

July

S	M	T	W	T	F	S
		1	2	3	4	5
6	7	8	9	10	11	12
13	14	15	16	17	18	19
20	21	22	23	24	25	26
27	28	29	30	31		

August

S	M	T	W	T	F	S
					1	2
3	4	5	6	7	8	9
10	11	12	13	14	15	16
17	18	19	20	21	22	23
24	25	26	27	28	29	30
31						

September

S	M	T	W	T	F	S
	1	2	3	4	5	6
7	8	9	10	11	12	13
14	15	16	17	18	19	20
21	22	23	24	25	26	27
28	29	30				

October

S	M	T	W	T	F	S
			1	2	3	4
5	6	7	8	9	10	11
12	13	14	15	16	17	18
19	20	21	22	23	24	25
26	27	28	29	30	31	

November

S	M	T	W	T	F	S
						1
2	3	4	5	6	7	8
9	10	11	12	13	14	15
16	17	18	19	20	21	22
23	24	25	26	27	28	29
30						

December

S	M	T	W	T	F	S
	1	2	3	4	5	6
7	8	9	10	11	12	13
14	15	16	17	18	19	20
21	22	23	24	25	26	27
28	29	30	31			

DON'T BE CAUGHT ABACK!

Next year has more dates and new facts

Each edition of *The Mariner's Book of Days* contains different information of interest and concern to the mariner, adding substance to an encyclopedia of fact, legend, and lore. The unique reference value of the material deserves a place on any bookshelf when the work of the calendar is done. We invite you to ensure that you receive your new copy. Send us your order for *The Mariner's Book of Days 2008* and receive it in plenty of time to plan the year ahead.

Please send ________copies of *The Mariner's Book of Days 2008* to:

Name____

Address____

____

City/State/Zip_______________________________________

Price per copy is $13.95. Two or more copies are $12.00 each.
Please include $5.50 for shipping for the first copy, plus $1.50 for each additional copy.
New York State residents, please add sales tax.

Mail your order to:
Sheridan House Inc.
145 Palisade Street
Dobbs Ferry, NY 10522
www.sheridanhouse.com

Or Call Toll-Free 1-888-SHERIBK (743-7425)
AmEx, VISA, MasterCard, Discover are welcome.
Fax your credit card order to 1-914-693-0776
E-mail your credit card order to: orders@sheridanhouse.com
Payment must be in U.S. funds, payable on a U.S. bank.